Good News *for* Tough Times

Good News *for* Tough Times

Mort Crim

SERVANT PUBLICATIONS
ANN ARBOR, MICHIGAN

Vine Books is an imprint of Servant Publications especially designed to serve evangelical Christians.

Scripture quotations marked NIV are taken from the HOLY BIBLE, NEW INTERNATIONAL VERSION®. Copyright 1973, 1978, 1984 by International Bible Society. Used by permission of Zondervan Publishing House. All rights reserved. Verses marked NRSV are from the New Revised Standard Version of the Bible, copyrighted 1989 by the Division of Christian Education of the National Council of Churches of Christ in the USA. Used by permission. All rights reserved. Verses marked RSV are from the Revised Standard Version of the Bible, copyrighted 1946, 1952, 1971 by the Division of Christian Education of the National Council of Churches of Christ in the USA. Used by permission. Verses marked NLT are taken from the *Holy Bible*, New Living Translation, copyright 1996. Used by permission of Tyndale House Publishers, Inc., Wheaton, Illinois 60189. All rights reserved. Verses marked NJB are taken from the New Jerusalem Bible, copyright 1985 by Darton, Longman & Todd Ltd and Doubleday. All rights reserved.

Published by Servant Publications
P.O. Box 8617
Ann Arbor, Michigan 48107

Cover design by Eric Walljasper
Author Photograph: Bob Foran, Ann Arbor, Mich.

02 03 04 10 9 8 7 6 5 4 3 2 1

Printed in the United States of America
ISBN 1-56955-247-9

Library of Congress Cataloging-in-Publication Data

Crim, Mort.
    Good news for tough times / Mort Crim.
        p. cm.
    ISBN 1-56955-247-9 (alk. paper)
    1. Christian life. I. Title.
    BV4501.3 .C75 2002
    242'.4—dc21

                                                          2001008004

To
Paul Harvey

Friend, mentor, and America's greatest storyteller
since Will Rogers

Preface

Good News for Tough Times sounds like a title for today. It is.

But the title would have seemed just as appropriate in the 1980s, to a generation struggling with its own unemployment, economic uncertainty, and threats to world peace.

Or in the 1960s, to a nation wrenched by war in Vietnam, turmoil on its campuses, and race riots in its cities.

Or during all the cold war years, when U.S. and Soviet missiles held each nation hostage and the potential annihilation of civilization could be measured in minutes.

Tough times aren't new. They're as modern as terrorists flying jetliners into buildings and spreading lethal toxins. But they're also as ancient as cavemen fighting off wild animals, starvation, and disease.

Good news isn't new either. It tends to speak in a quieter voice than bad news and, therefore, doesn't get as much attention. But in every generation, behind every tragedy and crisis, there's an abundance of personal heroism, courage, and kindness just waiting to be discovered.

The *tougher* the times, the more important it is that we make the discovery. That we find reasons for hope, confidence, and optimism.

As a journalist I've discovered such reasons in the simple, everyday experiences of ordinary people. A catastrophe such as the terrorist attacks on September 11 only dramatizes the basic goodness in people—it doesn't create it. Disasters reveal heroes—they don't make them.

America is a land rich with decency and awash in good news. That's why my daily radio series, *Second Thoughts*, will never run out of material. After eight years of broadcasting nearly three thousand reports about good people doing good things, I've only scratched the surface. Good news is happening faster than I can write about it.

Many of the people whose stories appear in these pages are motivated by a deep, religious faith. For some, this faith finds its expression through an established religious tradition. For others, it is more private and personal.

The common thread through all these accounts is *action*. These are not stories about abstract theological or philosophical concepts. They are about beliefs that move mountains. That get things done. That empower. That overcome obstacles. That make life better for others.

It's conventional wisdom that news reporting eventually turns journalists into cynics. My experience has been just the opposite. Seeing so much good in the world, observing incredible love and sacrifice, has strengthened my faith—not only in people but in the Creator who designed this universe.

I believe the really good news for these tough times is that we are not alone in the universe. That God exists, that he loves us, and that in him we can find both strength and serenity. As the writer of the Psalms expressed it:

When I am afraid,
I will trust in you.
In God, whose word I praise,

in God I trust; I will not be afraid.
What can mortal man do to me?

PSALM 56:3-4, NIV

But faith is a very personal matter. No one is argued into it or out of it. Some readers may be disappointed to discover that nowhere in this book is there an *argument* for believing in a higher power.

However, if you read carefully between the lines, I think you'll discover in these stories, as I have, unmistakable hints of God working in the world through people who often aren't even aware of it.

Acknowledgments

My life and work have been influenced by so many people it is impossible to recognize all of them on these pages. But the following deserve special mention:

First, the people whose lives I've written about and whose personal stories are the basis for this book. They are responsible for whatever inspiration, wisdom, or understanding is contained in these essays.

Paul Harvey and his wife, Lynne (Angel), for taking time to counsel me about life and career when, as a young college student, I sought their advice. And for later placing confidence in me to be Paul's vacation substitute. Writing and delivering *Paul Harvey News* from 1980 to 1984 provided important preparation for the national radio programs I'm doing today. Paul was a major reason I went into broadcasting, and his continuing role as mentor and friend is appreciated.

Ron Gorski, Paul Harvey's newsroom producer, who became my colleague during those substitution years and whose expertise and friendship are still valued.

Tom O'Brien, my former boss at ABC radio, whose genius as a news manager I've only fully appreciated in retrospect. And Nick George, Tom's managing editor, who taught me more about good radio writing than all my professors. (To this day, I cannot bring myself to call a *ship* a *vessel.*)

Bert Ghezzi, my friend and editor, who months before the tragic events of September 11 had suggested the title for this third in our series of *Good News* books. How could we have suspected at that time just how tough life would become for all of us?

Cindy Carney, my kind and capable assistant, who accepted the daunting challenge of initially selecting these scripts from the nearly three thousand I'd written for my daily radio series, *Second Thoughts*. She managed to do this while still handling my speaking and traveling schedule and keeping our office running with both efficiency and good humor.

Terry Oprea, Jeff Tottis, Joanne Froh, Lisa Hubbs, Tim Hinkle, Greg Zonca, and the entire radio team at Mort Crim Communications, as well as Dave Scott, Laurie Lounsbury, Bill Vogel, and their team at the Michigan Talk Radio Network. These pleasant professionals make it a joy to produce our radio programs—even in *tough times*.

The Reverends Conrad Sharps, Norman Pritchard, and Bruce Rigdon for providing regular inspiration from the pulpit. Each possesses that rare ability to combine good theology with relevancy and common sense.

Longtime friends Steve and Joyce Bell, Bill and Gloria Gaither, Dick and Alyssa Mertz, John and Kitty Burrows, and Vince and Frankie Leonard, who are always there for conversation, counsel, and encouragement.

My son, Al, who has quietly contributed enormously to this book and to my radio series by researching stories and statistics as well as suggesting theme and direction for certain pieces.

My daughter, Carey, who cannot imagine how much her constant love, optimism, and wise advice have helped me through my own most difficult challenges. She possesses her late mother's talents for compassion and clarity.

Of all my children's accomplishments, it is their solid values and strong commitment to make a positive difference in the world that make me most proud and most hopeful for their future.

Finally, my deep and undying gratitude to Renee. A person is indeed fortunate to find love once in a lifetime. I have found it twice. Renee's consistent support, enthusiasm for life, sense of humor, tolerance for my faults and failings, and most of all, her love, are more appreciated than she can know.

The Survivor

*I*n the early hours after terrorists took down New York's World Trade Center, an old man was pulled from the rubble, wounded and in shock. As rescuers brushed debris from his clothing, some began to recognize him—even though soot had turned his snow-white beard a dirty gray.

"This isn't the first time they've tried to kill me," the old man told a reporter.

"You think you were the target?" she asked.

"Oh, no doubt about it. All these thousands of dead and missing don't matter to the terrorists. I'm the one they were after. You see, my enemies have been trying to kill me ever since I was born."

The old man's eyes were kind, but steeled with resolve. The reporter thought he looked remarkably fit for somebody his age.

"In the early 1900s, I enlisted in a war some thought would end all wars," he recounted. "It didn't. And in 1941, they hit me in my own backyard. Well, nothing galvanizes this old man like a direct attack. Especially from someone who wants to destroy my way of life. Let me tell you, that's never going to happen!"

His voice grew stronger. "Ma'am, you have no idea how many times they thought I was too timid, or had grown too soft to fight back. How many times they've mistaken my tolerance for weakness. I've survived Korea, Vietnam, the Persian Gulf, city riots, campus turmoil, assassinations, impeachments, and more family fights than I can count.

"And these murdering cowards—these tinhorn terrorists—think they can bring me down? Just be patient, and you'll see how tough—how resilient—this old man is. You'll see kids playing soccer again. Teachers teaching. Doctors healing. Factories producing. People shopping.

"And you'll see some of my finest and bravest young people fanning out to catch these criminals and to keep America safe as a beacon of democracy and hope. It won't be easy. And we will have to become more thoughtful. More aware of the poverty, injustice, and hate that breed terrorism. More committed to those who suffer. But compassion is in my soul, so I'm confident we'll do that, too."

"Just one more question," the reporter said. "Are you a religious person?"

The old man laughed, pulled a crumpled dollar bill from his wallet, and pointed to the words, "In God We Trust." "That's another thing they don't understand," he said, "these folks who want to kill me. You see, I've never been one to wear faith or patriotism on my sleeve. But in times of crisis, they boil up and burst forth like a volcano."

At that moment, a rescue worker walked up and handed the old man a crumpled top hat. "Sir," he said, "I think this is yours."

The red, white, and blue were barely visible beneath the dust. The brim was singed around the edges. But the old man straightened it out, brushed it off, and placed it proudly on his head.

"I'm going to be just fine," he said to the reporter. "Tell them we're all going to be just fine, will you?"

As word of the survivor spread, rescuers planted a big American flag right in the middle of the devastation.

So the whole world could see, so the whole world would know, that the old man was alive; Uncle Sam was stronger than ever.

The Lord is my light and my salvation—
whom shall I fear?
The Lord is the stronghold of my life—
of whom shall I be afraid?
When evil men advance against me
to devour my flesh,
When my enemies and my foes attack me,
they will stumble and fall.
Though an army besiege me,
my heart will not fear;
though war break out against me,
even then will I be confident.

PSALM 27:1-3, NIV

Good Grief

Nothing speaks our grief so well as to speak nothing.

RICHARD CRASHAW

*H*ave you ever been in the position of trying to comfort a person in the midst of his or her grief? Most of us have been or will be. It's one of the most important roles any good friend can play, but sometimes also one of the toughest. Often, we feel helpless in such a situation. What should we say? What words can we find that will fit?

The best advice comes from those who've been on the receiving end of such attempts to comfort. People like Joseph Bayly. Three of his children died over the course of just a few years. In his book, *A View From a Hearse,* he recalls sitting in the funeral home after losing one of his children. A man came over and talked to him. He spoke of life's mystery and of how and why such tragedies occur. Joseph said he knew what the man was saying was all true, but it irritated him. He just wished this friend would disappear.

Eventually the man did leave and someone else moved in to sit beside Joseph. This friend said nothing. Didn't interrogate. Didn't offer advice. Didn't try to explain. Didn't ask any questions. He just sat there, silently, feeling Joseph's pain and empathizing with his loss. Joseph Bayly remembers that he was sorry to see that friend go.

Sometimes we help a person most when we speak the least. In times of grief, the greatest comfort comes not from eloquence but from empathy.

Love ... bears all things, believes all things, hopes all things, endures all things.

1 CORINTHIANS 13:4-7, NRSV

The Gift of Determination

I knew my friend John was a determined, tough old bird, but I never appreciated just how tough until the chips were down. Chemotherapy had left his heart so weakened doctors told him he couldn't survive the one surgical procedure that might save his life.

Instead of crawling off somewhere to die, John forced himself to walk every day, fighting fatigue and facing down discouragement. Finally, he reached his goal of three miles a day. To the amazement of his physicians, his heart had strengthened so significantly that he was able to undergo the procedure, and today he seems well on his way to full recovery.

Some people say that we all can do more than we think we can. Yet I think it's the other way around: We can do only what we think we can. Like Marty Ravellette: he kicked open the window of a burning car and rescued a trapped woman. This despite the fact Marty was born with no arms. But when he saw an eighty-six-year-old woman about to burn to death, Marty knew he had to act, and he did.

Sometimes it takes a crisis for us to recognize what incredible potential we possess. I am amazed at just how *much* return some people are able to get on limited assets. If the rest of us could learn to use just a *little* of what's available to us, the results would be remarkable.

There are different kinds of gifts, but the same Spirit.... Now to each one the manifestation of the Spirit is given for the common good.

1 CORINTHIANS 12:4, 7, NIV

Change Your Mind

> The greatest discovery of my generation is that man can alter his life simply by altering his attitude of mind.
>
> WILLIAM JAMES

*T*here really are only two ways to make your life better: One is to change the situation. The other is to change the way you look at it. Sometimes we can't change the circumstances, but we can always adjust our viewpoint.

A Little Leaguer apparently had that figured out. A neighbor overheard him talking to himself as he strutted through his backyard, wearing his baseball uniform and toting a ball and bat.

"I'm the greatest hitter in the world," he announced, tossing the ball into the air, swinging at it, and missing.

"Strike one," he yelled. Then he repeated the process.

"I'm the greatest hitter in the world," he told himself again, once more tossing the ball into the air, swinging at it, and missing it. "Strike two," he shouted.

Again he yelled, "I'm the greatest hitter in the world."

When he missed for the third time, the little fellow adjusted his hat, spit on his hands, rubbed them together triumphantly, and shouted, "Strike three. Wow. I'm the greatest *pitcher* in the world!"

Sometimes we can change our circumstances. Sometimes we can change only our attitude. More often than we think, that's enough.

Let the renewing of your minds transform you, so that you may discern for yourselves what is the will of God—what is good and acceptable and mature.

ROMANS 12:2, NJB

Defusing Anger

> *The happiness of a man in this life does not consist in the absence, but in the mastery, of his passions.*
>
> ALFRED, LORD TENNYSON

We've all had some experience of road rage. They have it in England, too, where Robbie Crawford admits that he was one of the worst. If a driver cut him off, his temper would boil. Well, he knew that wasn't healthy, not for him or others on the road, so he reformed. And he decided to do something about the problem.

Robbie designed an electronic display for the rear window of cars. It flashes messages such as "Thank You" and "Sorry." They're already selling big in Scotland, and eventually he hopes to market the signs in Italy, Germany, Australia, and the United States.

Road rage may be a fairly recent phenomenon, but rage has been around as long as the human race. Once when Abraham Lincoln heard a friend speak with great anger about someone, Lincoln advised the man to pour all of his hostility into a letter.

The friend took the suggestion and brought the completed letter to Lincoln. The president praised the man for his articulate severity.

The writer then asked Lincoln, "How would you advise me to send it?" Lincoln replied, "Send it? Oh, I wouldn't send it. I sometimes write letters like this. It does me good. But I never send them."

We all get angry, and at times we should. What's important is that we find constructive outlets for that anger, whether it's an electronic sign in the rear window, the letter we never mail, or the golf balls we smash with a vengeance.

We've been told, "Don't get mad—get even." Yet getting mad only at the right thing at the right time and for the right reason is OK. Rage and outrage are destructive only when misdirected.

> *A mild answer turns away wrath,*
>   *sharp words stir up anger....*
> *The hot-headed provokes disputes,*
>   *the equable allays dissension.*

PROVERBS 15:1, 18, NJB

Deceiving Looks

> *If you judge people, you have no time to love them.*
>
> MOTHER TERESA OF CALCUTTA

*D*avid Sims and his family had gone to the park to watch their daughter play softball. At a picnic table, near the highway, David noticed a man in dirty clothes, his possessions stuffed into a shopping cart.

For a moment it appeared the man was about to walk toward them. David tried not to notice. To his relief, the man was only going to the drinking fountain.

As the man lingered at the fountain, watching the girls play ball, David studied him. How had he gotten this way? Did he have kids? What had forced him onto the street?

At the edge of the park, David's young sons were playing kickball. David was too absorbed in the softball game to pay attention until, suddenly, he heard the nine-year-old scream at his three-year-old brother, "Erik, stop!"

David turned to see little Erik chasing the ball toward the highway. Cars whizzed by. David raced toward the road. But the man in the dirty clothes already had reached the boy, and snatched him to safety just seconds before one speeding car most certainly would have struck him.

Only a short while before, David had tried to pretend this man didn't exist. Amazing, isn't it, how quickly our view of another person can change? It's not only in sports that someone can be transformed—instantly—from bum to hero.

Do not judge, and you will not be judged; because the judgments you give are the judgments you will get, and the standard you use will be the standard used for you.

MATTHEW 7:1-2, NJB

The Way of Forgiveness

> *A wise man will make haste to forgive,*
> *because he knows the true value of time,*
> *and will not suffer it to pass away in unnec-*
> *essary pain.*
>
> SAMUEL JOHNSON

I'm a sucker for napkins with slogans, the ones offering such sage aphorisms as: Money isn't everything, but it sure keeps the kids in touch. Or my wife's favorite: The Queen Doesn't Cook. Yesterday I saw one that didn't make me smile, but it did make me think. It read: To err is human. To forgive, unthinkable.

Forgiveness was unthinkable to Everett Worthington Jr. after an intruder bludgeoned his seventy-eight-year-old mother to death. He was so angry he looked at a baseball bat and thought, "If I could find that guy, I'd beat his brains out."

Then he realized that such a thought made *his* heart as dark as that of the intruder. Eventually, Worthington was able to let go of the hate and actually reach a state of forgiveness. In his book, *To Forgive Is Human: How to Put Your Past in the Past,* he outlines five steps that led him to forgiveness:

1. Recall the hurt, relive the pain, acknowledge that the offense was committed.
2. Empathize with the offender. Try to understand the motivations.
3. Recognize that forgiveness is a gift. You don't earn it.
4. Make a commitment to forgiveness.
5. Hold on to forgiveness. Don't give up on it.

Worthington says even following these five steps, forgiveness can't be rushed. Grief always has to come first. "Forgiveness," he said, "is the fragrance the violet sheds on the heel that has crushed it."

If you forgive those who sin against you, your heavenly Father will forgive you. But if you refuse to forgive others, your Father will not forgive your sins.

MATTHEW 6:14-15, NLT

Eternal Vigilance

> *Eternal vigilance is the price, not only of liberty, but of a great many other things. It is the price of everything that is good. It is the price of one's own soul.*
>
> WOODROW WILSON

*T*he briefest lapse in attention can produce tragedy that lasts a lifetime. How many people are in prison because of a single moment of anger? How many car accidents have resulted from one act of carelessness or from one second of negligence? Ironically, the longer we live without disaster, the more vulnerable we become to smugness and apathy.

As a pilot, I'm always intrigued by aircraft accident reports citing pilot error by someone who's logged thousands of hours. Experience alone is no guarantee against complacency. It may even promote it.

A veteran sea captain once wrote these words:

When anyone asks me how I can best describe my experience in nearly forty years at sea, I merely say, "uneventful." In all my experience I have never been in any accident. I have seen but one vessel in distress in all my years at sea. I never saw a wreck and never have been wrecked nor was I ever in any predicament that threatened to end in disaster of any sort.

Those words were written in 1907 by E.J. Smith, captain of the *Titanic.*

In our kind of world, there's no substitute for keeping our heads up and our eyes open. Vigilance *is* the price of liberty and of a whole lot more.

Therefore keep watch, because you do not know on what day your Lord will come. But understand this: If the owner of the house had known at what time of night the thief was coming, he would have kept watch and would not have let his house be broken into. So you also must be ready, because the Son of Man will come at an hour when you do not expect him.
MATTHEW 24:42-44, NIV

Fire Extinguisher

> Wise men never sit and wail their loss, but cheerily seek how to redress their harms.
>
> WILLIAM SHAKESPEARE

Los Angeles firefighters know about gang violence. More than once, they've responded to a blaze only to face another danger—hostile crowds, including gang members seething with anger.

Many distrust the very institutions charged with serving and protecting them. So, some L.A. firefighters decided to do something more than sit around the station houses playing cards and waiting for an alarm. They opened the doors of their fire stations to the communities. They specifically sought out leaders of eight gangs. Then they introduced themselves at gang intervention meetings.

The gang members responded. When firefighters invited them to join a toy drive, they responded with enthusiasm, which shouldn't be surprising. Many youngsters who join gangs are inherently good kids. They're just kids with no other support system. They don't have caring families. So they turn to gangs for a sense of belonging and a sense of worth.

Now in Los Angeles some gang members show up on fire runs, helping to protect the firefighters they used to assault.

What began as a simple opening of doors has mushroomed into book donations, tutoring, character-building picnics, and career days. All because some firefighters recognized a duty beyond their job description.

Maybe we can't do much about violence raging in distant places, but each of us has power to extinguish small blazes of prejudice and misunderstanding that may be burning in our own communities.

Love ... keeps no record of when it has been wronged. It is never glad about injustice but rejoices whenever the truth wins out.

1 CORINTHIANS 13:5-6, NLT

Infectious Love

> *The golden rule is of no use whatsoever unless
> you realize that it is YOUR move.*
>
> FRANK CRANE

*R*ashad Williams was fifteen, an age when
most boys are thinking about girls, or
sports, or just hanging out with other guys. Yet Rashad couldn't
stop thinking about Lance Kirklin, one of the students brutally
wounded in that murderous high school shooting rampage
near Denver. Lance had been shot several times, once in the
face, and he had to learn to walk again.

Rashad had seen reports that Lance's family had no medical insurance and that the boy's medical bills could grow to a
million dollars. What could one fifteen-year-old possibly do?
Rashad didn't have money, but he did have two strong legs.
He decided to run in San Francisco's annual seven-and-a-half-
mile Bay to Breakers race. He would ask people to pledge
money for every mile completed. Maybe he could raise a few
hundred dollars.

When a newspaper columnist printed the story, however,
donations began pouring in. Not just a few hundred dollars,
but thousands—eighteen thousand dollars in all.

We often wonder, *What can one person do?* Then someone

comes along with an answer. Some adolescent does something to remind us that one good deed is like a single rock rolling down a mountain. As it gains momentum, it can become an avalanche, eventually enveloping an entire community in a blanket of goodwill.

Charity is like a cold. It's tough to be exposed to it without catching it.

In everything do to others as you would have them do to you.
MATTHEW 7:12, NRSV

Say Thanks

One day, William Stidger, a professor at Boston University, began thinking about all the people throughout his life who had helped, nurtured, and encouraged him, and he realized that he hadn't taken the time to thank them all.

One stood out especially in Stidger's mind, a schoolteacher from many years before who'd gone out of her way to inspire in him a love of poetry. He didn't know if she was even still alive, but his appreciation for what she'd done was so powerful that he wrote her a letter of thanks, hoping that somehow it would reach her.

It did. And this was the reply he received:

My dear Willie,
I cannot tell you how much your note meant to me. I am in my eighties, living alone in a small room, cooking my own meals, lonely and, like the last leaf of autumn, lingering behind. You will be interested to know that I taught school for fifty years and yours is the first note of

appreciation I ever received. It came on a blue-cold morning and it cheered me as nothing has in many years.

It had also been many years since anyone had called William Stidger "Willie." He's a bit bald now, and over fifty. But as he read his teacher's letter, he discovered he was still not too old to cry.

Who are the *un*thanked people in our lives? Could this be the day we were always planning to get around to, someday, to say thanks?

So give encouragement to each other, and keep strengthening one another, as you do already.

1 THESSALONIANS 5:11, NJB

Vertical Coffins

> *Wondrous is the strength of cheerfulness and its power of endurance. The cheerful man will do more in the same time, will do it better, and will persevere in it longer, than the sad or sullen.*
>
> THOMAS CARLYLE

*T*here's nothing particularly inspiring about a tollbooth. You know how it is. You toss your change into a basket. Or, if you don't have change, you hand your dollar bill to the toll taker, who may seem bored, and why not? After all, that's got to be the most uninteresting, unexciting job in the world. Nothing to do but watch this monotonous string of cars pass.

So it really caught one driver's attention when he heard happy music blaring from a particular booth and inside saw a young man, jumping and jiving and spinning around—clearly having a great time.

The motorist was something of a student of human behavior, so he had to ask the young man, "How can you be so happy in such a humdrum job?" Easy, the young man explained. That tollbooth could be nothing more than a vertical coffin. For eight hours he could just stand or sit there, his brain on hold, while he went through the motions. That, he said, is death. He would have none of it.

This young man plans to be a dancer someday, so he's practicing. And that makes this otherwise boring job a great job. Think about it, he said: "I have a private office with a view of the Golden Gate Bridge, a place where half the Western world vacations, and every day I dance. It doesn't get any better."

If you're feeling boxed in, break out. Turn your vertical coffin into a dance studio.

Rejoice in the Lord always. I will say it again: Rejoice!

PHILIPPIANS 4:4, NIV

Thanks for Trouble

When God shuts a door he opens a window.
HUGH CASSON AND JOYCE GRENFELL

*D*o you envy people who are able to find something positive in every negative experience? Actually, this isn't just some natural ability. It's learned. We can teach ourselves to take life's setbacks, turn them right side up, and recognize their value.

Start with the fact that we don't have everything we want. Sounds like a negative, doesn't it? But looked at another way, not having everything we want gives us something to work for. Something to look forward to. What kind of life would it be if we had nothing good to anticipate?

We can be thankful that we don't know everything. Turned right side up, this lack of knowledge becomes an opportunity to learn.

Difficult times? These provide us a chance to grow.

Limitations? Opportunities for improvement.

New challenges? These build strength and character.

Mistakes? Yes, our mistakes can be assets. If we use them wisely, they can teach us valuable lessons.

Even fatigue can be a positive, because when we're tired and worn out it means that somehow, some way, we've made a difference.

It doesn't take much thought to be thankful for the good things in life. But it takes a special kind of wisdom to appreciate the value of trouble.

Give thanks in all circumstances; for this is the will of God in Christ Jesus for you.

1 THESSALONIANS 5:18, NRSV

Laughing at Failure

When we can begin to take our failures nonseriously, it means we are ceasing to be afraid of them. It is of immense importance to learn to laugh at ourselves.

KATHERINE MANSFIELD

*I*f anyone ever had a right to wear the label "failure," he did. As a child, he was sexually abused. At the age of eight, his father died. As a young adult, he drifted aimlessly from job to job and town to town. He tried school, but flunked out of Kent State, and he fought such serious bouts of depression that he twice tried to kill himself.

Much was missing from the life of this desperate young man, including discipline. That changed when, at age twenty-two, having tried just about everything else, he joined the Marine Corps. His four years in uniform instilled in him a sense of responsibility.

When he returned to civilian life, he began reading self-help books. And he developed another quality he'd never had—a sense of humor. In fact, he liked being funny so much that he bought a book of jokes and managed to get a job writing one-liners for a disc jockey in Cleveland.

That led to a five-year stint on the comedy club circuit and then to national television. Today, unless someone told you, you'd never guess that the great comic success Drew Carey spent the first part of his life as such a failure.

Learning to laugh at trouble may help us face it. It certainly guarantees that we'll never run out of things to amuse us.

> *O Lord my God, I called to you for help*
> *and you healed me.*
> *O Lord, you brought me up from the grave;*
> *you spared me from going down into the pit.*
>
> PSALM 30:2–3, NIV

The Cost of Hate

> *The price of hating other human beings is loving oneself less.*
>
> ELDRIDGE CLEAVER

*M*y mother grew up in Missouri, so I know a little something about the Missouri mule, famed for stubbornness. When mother was a girl, the mule was still being used to till the land. Occasionally, a farmer could be just as hardheaded as his mule.

A visitor leaned on the fence and watched with great interest as one old farmer seemed to be having considerable difficulty getting his mule to pull the plow. Finally the visitor said, "You know, I don't like to tell you how to run your business, but you wouldn't have to work nearly so hard if you'd just say 'gee' and 'haw' to that mule instead of tugging so much on those lines."

The old farmer stopped, pulled a big handkerchief from his pocket, and wiped his face. Then he said, "Reckon you're right. But this mule kicked me five years ago and I ain't spoke to him since."

Sometimes it's hard to let go of a grudge, even when it's in our own self-interest. However, grudges don't hurt others. They hurt only us. Still, no matter how difficult we make it on ourselves, we're determined to just keep pulling on those reins until we die.

A grudge is one of the heaviest loads anyone can carry. The people who hate you inevitably will be the losers—unless, of course, you hate them back.

Bear with each other and forgive whatever grievances you may have against one another.

COLOSSIANS 3:13, NIV

Life's Paradoxes

> *The only things we ever keep*
> *Are what we give away.*
>
> LOUIS GINZBERG

When tragedy strikes, we discover what's important to us.

During the rash of brushfires in Florida, thousands of residents were forced to leave their homes. Asked by reporters what they had chosen to take with them, their stories were strikingly similar. Photographs inevitably headed the list. Then, sentimental keepsakes. Treasures insurance could never replace. Symbols of life's most memorable moments. Reminders of shared love and of lost loved ones.

In his inspirational book *To Remind*, former Nebraska senator Carl Curtis tells about an old couple about to retire. The small cottage they'd purchased wouldn't hold all the furniture from their big farmhouse. So they called in their children, allowing them to take all the unneeded furniture.

During the night, fire broke out. The elderly couple escaped, unhurt, but the house and everything in it were destroyed. As they gazed at the dying embers, the old man placed his arm around his wife and said, "You know, the only things we have left are what we gave away."

Ultimately, the most valuable treasures any of us will possess are those we give away. It's one of life's great paradoxes that—in the end—these are the only treasures we're permitted to keep.

Anyone who wants to save his life will lose it; but anyone who loses his life for my sake, will save it.

LUKE 9:24, NJB

One Eye Open

*T*he speaker was addressing a management group and he got a knowing laugh when he declared, "Only the paranoid survive." It was clear he didn't mean for his cynical overstatement to be taken literally—only that in today's fast-paced, competitive, high-risk society, business leaders do have to stay on their toes. What is required isn't paranoia, but vigilance.

Perhaps we could learn from the birds. Birds have demonstrated an ability to sleep with one eye open and half their brain awake. Research has now proven that birds possess this unique talent, and they're especially good at it when there are predators around.

How do they sleep and stay awake at the same time? Scientists at Indiana State University say they do it by using different parts of the brain. Their research leads them to believe that dolphins, seals, and manatees also can do this.

Learning to relax, to trust, to live life with an inner calm while at the same time remaining alert to danger is a difficult skill but one that's essential to survival. Fortunately, we don't have to be paranoid to survive in our kind of world. But we do have to keep one eye open.

Be sober, be watchful. Your adversary, the devil prowls around like a roaring lion, seeking some one to devour.

1 PETER 5:8, RSV

Optimism Is Divine

> *Think positively and masterfully, with confidence and faith, and life becomes more secure, more fraught with action, richer in achievement and experience.*
>
> EDDIE RICKENBACKER

Oscar Wilde once described a pessimist as one who, when faced with the choice of two evils, chooses both. Pessimism not only is bad for the personality, it's also harmful to one's health. Optimism, on the other hand, has incredible healing power.

My friend was facing the greatest medical challenge of his life. We'd gone to the hospital to cheer him up. The irony was that he ended up making us feel better. His optimism, his confidence that he'd beat the life-threatening illness, and his continuing enthusiasm were contagious. I don't know how much our visit helped him, but it certainly improved our mood. And ultimately, he did recover.

Robert Louis Stevenson, the great Scottish novelist and author of *Treasure Island*, spent much of his time confined to bed, yet illness never stifled his optimism. Once when his wife heard him coughing for several minutes, she said with some sarcasm, "I suppose you still believe it's a wonderful day."

Stevenson glanced at the rays of sunshine bouncing off the bedroom walls and replied, "I do. I'll never permit a row of medicine bottles to block my horizon." Few tonics are more effective in chasing away the shadows of life than the expectation that things will be better tomorrow.

Jesus looked at them and said to them, "With men this is impossible, but with God all things are possible."

MATTHEW 19:26, RSV

Peace of Mind

> *Order your soul; reduce your wants; live in charity; associate in Christian community; obey the laws; trust in Providence.*
>
> AUGUSTINE OF HIPPO

*T*here may not be a formula for producing peace of mind, but a study at Duke University does identify eight qualities that people who enjoy peace of mind seem to share:

1. Absence of suspicions and resentment. Nursing a grudge agitates the mind.
2. Living in the present. No one has peace of mind who is preoccupied with past mistakes and failures.
3. Not wasting time and energy fighting conditions that can't be changed.
4. Forcing yourself to stay involved. Not withdrawing during periods of emotional stress.
5. Refusing to indulge in self-pity when life hands you a raw deal. Accepting the fact that no one gets through life without some sorrow and misfortune.
6. Cultivating the old-fashioned virtues: love, honor, compassion, and loyalty.

7. Not expecting too much of yourself.
8. Finding something bigger than yourself to believe in. Self-centered, egotistical people always score lowest on the peace of mind scale.

Peace of mind is an interesting quality. It can't be purchased by the wealthiest person on earth, yet it's within reach of the poorest.

> *Never worry about anything; but tell God all your desires of every kind in prayer and petition shot through with gratitude, and the peace of God which is beyond our understanding will guard your hearts and thoughts in Christ Jesus.*
>
> PHILIPPIANS 4:6-7, NJB

Secret of Success

> Always bear in mind that your own resolution to success is more important than any other one thing.
>
> ABRAHAM LINCOLN

*M*y friend Dick is a businessman who seems to turn everything he touches into success. When I mentioned this to him, he laughed. "Did you know that about eight out of every ten of my ventures fail?" he said. "But you read only about my successes."

Another man in an earlier generation lost his job and the very same year was defeated in his bid for the legislature. A year later his business failed. Finally, he managed to win an election, but the very next year the woman he loved died. The following year he had a nervous breakdown, then suffered two more political defeats before finally winning a seat in Congress. Then he failed to be renominated and was defeated in a bid for the Senate. Later the man tried for nomination as vice president and failed. He made another run for the Senate and failed.

Yet, we don't remember that man for all those failures. No. We remember Abraham Lincoln for his one great success.

There's a big difference between failing at something and

being a failure. We're never total failures until we believe that we are.

> *Whenever you face trials of any kind, consider it nothing but joy, because you know that the testing of your faith produces endurance; and let endurance have its full effect, so that you may be mature and complete, lacking in nothing.*
>
> JAMES 1:2-4, NRSV

Strength in Weakness

> *Courage is the ladder on which all the other virtues mount.*
>
> CLARA BOOTH LUCE

To many people Mark McGwire became a hero when he broke Roger Maris' home run record. Yet McGwire's greatness transcends his impressive baseball skills. McGwire is outstanding for another reason: courage. The courage to acknowledge that once he required and sought psychotherapy.

In 1991, after a failed marriage and a dismal season at the plate, McGwire did what too many of us are unwilling to do—he went for help. That he then talked openly about it puts him in an even more exclusive league.

Norway's prime minister, Kjell Magne Bondevik, also became a member of that league by admitting to the world he had taken nearly a month's leave because of depression and work overload. Bondevik revealed that besides playing with his children and taking walks with his wife, he also had received professional counseling and that his health was steadily improving.

For much too long we've kept our mental and emotional problems in the closet. When sports heroes like Mark McGwire and political leaders like Prime Minister Bondevik are willing to be up front about their personal difficulties, it opens the door for others to let sunshine into the dark corners of their tortured existence.

It takes a strong person to acknowledge a weakness. Admitting our own fears and insecurities may be a supreme act of courage.

Confess your sins to one another, and pray for one another, so that you may be healed.

JAMES 5:16, NRSV

Your Finest Hour

> *If you want the rainbow, you gotta put up with the rain.*
>
> DOLLY PARTON

*H*ow do you learn to trust life again after a major disappointment? Or tragedy? One way is to look around. By studying the lives of those who've overcome, you'll recognize that wounds do heal and grief can give way to joy.

Is your job in jeopardy? Has someone walked out on you? Has your self-esteem been crushed? Is one of your children on a self-destructive path? Are you fighting a disease? Are you facing bankruptcy? Bad things do happen to good people.

Yet we can rekindle hope when we feel hopeless by looking around. We don't have to look far to discover people who've had it just as bad or worse. People who've survived the long night of despair and are now back in the emotional sunshine. People who can truly say of their tragedies, as Winston Churchill said of London's war years, "This was our finest hour."

The problem is that we rarely recognize our crises as "finest hours" until after the fact. I doubt Churchill felt so positive while German rockets were falling on Britain. So if you're in a tough spot, *look* around. Recognize that other people have made it and that you can, too. In time, you may recall this dark moment as your finest hour.

If your situation seems unusually tough right now, it may mean you're right on the verge of winning!

We also boast in our sufferings, knowing that suffering produces endurance, and endurance produces character, and character produces hope, and hope does not disappoint us, because God's love has been poured into our hearts through the Holy Spirit that has been given to us.

ROMANS 5:3-5, NRSV

The Best Christmas Gift

> *Salvation is not putting a man into heaven, but putting heaven into a man.*
>
> MALTBIE D. BABCOCK

*E*verybody knows the Salvation Army's bell-ringing Santas. We've all seen them collecting donations for the poor. But there was one little girl who knew the Army not for what it *collected*, but for what it *gave*.

A man was speaking at one of those Salvation Army street meetings. He was telling the crowd what his newfound faith had done in his life, how the Salvation Army had introduced him to God.

A heckler began shouting, "Why don't you shut up and sit down? Man, you're just dreaming."

Immediately, the heckler felt a tug on his coat. He looked down to see this little girl, who said:

"Sir, may I speak with you? That man talking is my daddy. He used to be a drunk. He spent all the money he made on whiskey. My mother was sad and cried a lot.

"Sometimes, when daddy *did* come home, he would hit my mother. I didn't have shoes or a nice dress for school. But look at my shoes. And see this dress? Daddy bought them for me.

"See, that's my mother over there—the woman with the

bright smile on her face. She even sings now when she's doing the laundry.

"Mister, if my daddy is dreaming, please don't wake him up."

Perhaps the proof of a person's faith is like the proof of a prescribed medicine: What does it really do for them?

"Why do you eat and drink with tax collectors and sinners?"
Jesus answered, "Those who are well have no need of a physi-
cian, but those who are sick; I have come to call not the righ-
teous but sinners to repentance."

LUKE 5:30-32, NRSV

Wait Training

*O*n his website, *Your Life Support System,* Steve Goodier tells of a man who was to meet his wife, who'd been shopping. They'd agreed on the time and place in the mall.

The man waited patiently for ten minutes. Then fifteen. But after half an hour, patience had given way to anger.

Nearby he spotted one of those photo booths where, for a few quarters, you can take four poses. The man sat down in the booth, deposited his coins, and assumed four of the most ferocious expressions he could manage. This wasn't too difficult. Then, he wrote his wife's name on the back of the pictures, handed them to a clerk, and said, "If you see a small, dark-haired lady who seems to be looking for someone, please give her these."

His wife saved those pictures. She carries them in her purse. Enough time has passed that both she and he can laugh about it. They both refer to the incident as his wait training.

Life provides all of us with wait training—waiting in line, waiting for traffic, waiting to hear about a new job, waiting for a medical report from the lab. Patience is more than a virtue in today's hypersonic world—it is an essential survival tool and a fundamental requirement for a happy life. And we have so many opportunities to practice it, we should be really good at it by now.

Be patient, therefore, beloved, until the coming of the Lord. The farmer waits for the precious crop from the earth, being patient with it until it receives the early and the late rains. You also must be patient.

JAMES 5:7-8, NRSV

When Opportunity Doesn't Knock

You don't just luck into things ... you build step by step, whether it's friendships or opportunities.

BARBARA BUSH

What do you do when you come up against a wall? I mean a wall too high to climb over, too wide to get around. What do you do when you've tried everything you can think of to scale that wall that's developed between you and your spouse? When you've exhausted every option trying to get past the job barriers that keep you from advancing, what do you do?

Sometimes you have to do what a good offensive line does in a football game. You have to create an opening. If you can't get over or around, maybe you'll just have to push through. But you have to be attuned to exactly the right opportunity:

A woman managed to get her call through to the CEO of a large firm. She said, "You were at a party Saturday night and you met a young woman in a navy blue dress. You talked to her for about half an hour."

The CEO said, "Yes, that's true."

"And," the woman continued, "You told her you were impressed with her knowledge and insight and that there might be a place for her on your staff, and you said to call you first thing this week."

"That's right," the CEO responded.

Then the caller said, "Well, I was listening to you both, and if she hasn't called, I'd like the job."

Opportunity doesn't always knock. Sometimes it simply stands quietly on the steps, waiting for us to open the door.

Be cunning as snakes and yet innocent as doves.

MATTHEW 10:16, NJB

Upgraded

> *Today is not yesterday; how can our works and thoughts, if they are always to be the fittest, continue always the same? Change, indeed, is painful, yet ever needful.*
>
> THOMAS CARLYLE

When Renee and I married, I inherited a stepson who programs computers for a living. There was a two-way benefit to this: I could learn from Jeff what RAM, CPU fan, and processor speed meant. And he could learn from me what "high-tech illiterate" meant.

On his first visit, Jeff checked out my system. Once he'd stopped laughing, he suggested I use that old, obsolete computer as a doorstop or a boat anchor. Couldn't I just donate it to charity, I wondered? No one, he assured me, was that desperate.

If I insisted on keeping it, at least it needed a memory upgrade to handle today's programs. With an investment of my money and Jeff's time, the old computer did take on a new life. It didn't *look* any different. Same keyboard. Same screen and printer. Same mouse. But changing the computer's innards changed everything.

On second thought, doesn't significant change always occur

on the inside? Good health programs don't focus on appearance. They concentrate on stress reduction and cardiovascular improvement. We can change clothes, hairstyles, jobs, cars, and even spouses. Yet we improve performance only with an inside upgrade.

Cosmetics are no substitute for content. Improving ourselves is like upgrading our computers. It requires a change on the inside.

> *I will give you a new heart and put a new spirit in you; I will remove from you your heart of stone and give you a heart of flesh. And I will put my Spirit in you and move you to follow my decrees and be careful to keep my laws.*
>
> EZEKIEL 36:26-27, NIV

The Right Choice

> *We are the choices we have made.*
>
> MERYL STREEP

*I*t was her dream job. She'd wanted it for as long as she could remember. But the job wasn't offered and finally the woman agreed to work for another firm. Then, less than a week before she was to start, the first company—the one where she'd always wanted to work—*did* offer her that dream job.

For this woman it was a dilemma because her integrity was as remarkable as her ability. And she had made a commitment. It wasn't on paper, but what did legalities have to do with obligation?

It was painful, but her decision was obvious. She rejected the ideal position in order to keep her word. That occurred twenty-two years ago. Today, she says it was the best decision she's ever made. The job she kept turned out to be terrific. Her colleagues, wonderful. She can't imagine that the job of her dreams could have been as rewarding.

As for the other company, it was acquired in a merger two years later and eventually was moved to another state.

Doing the right thing for the right reason may be harder in

the short run. Yet living with the consequences usually is easier in the long run. Bad decisions rarely produce good results.

You have already been told what is right
and what Yahweh wants of you.
Only this, to do what is right,
to love loyalty
and to walk humbly with your God.

MICAH 6:8, NJB

Smoke Signals

> *All things can be done by importunate prayer. It surmounts or removes all obstacles, overcomes every resisting force, and gains its ends in the face of invincible hindrances.*
>
> E.M. BOUNDS

*T*he ship had sunk and he was the only survivor. Tired and discouraged, he finally was washed ashore on a small, uninhabited island. He was a man of religious faith, so he prayed feverishly for God to rescue him. Every day he scanned the horizon but nothing came.

Exhausted, he eventually managed to build a small hut out of driftwood, a place to protect him from the weather and to store his few possessions.

But one day, after scavenging for food, he arrived back at his tiny hut to find it in flames. The worst had happened. Lightning had struck the dry wood. As smoke rolled into the sky, the man realized that everything was lost. He was stunned and angry. This time when he prayed, he cried out, "God, how could you do this to me?"

The next morning, he was awakened by the sound of a ship approaching the island. It had come to rescue him. As he was pulled aboard the boat that had been dispatched to the island, he asked, "How did you know I was here?"

One of the rescuers replied, "Oh, we saw your smoke signal."

What seems the worst thing that ever happened to you may turn out to be the best. History has 20-20 vision, and often it's only in retrospect that we really understand what's good for us.

"Because he loves me," says the Lord, "I will rescue him;
I will protect him, for he acknowledges my name.
He will call upon me, and I will answer him;
I will be with him in trouble."

PSALM 91:14-15, NIV

Personal Checkup

> When you know you are doing the very best
> within the circumstances of your existence,
> applaud yourself!
>
> RUSTY BERKUS

*T*here are many ways to evaluate our own progress in life. This is the story of one person's way that was—to say the least—unique.

The man waiting for the phone booth wasn't trying to listen, but he couldn't help overhearing the young man's end of the conversation.

"I'd like to talk to the boss. Are you the boss? Well, how would you like to hire a new gofer, somebody who's really on his toes? Oh, the one you've already got is doing a good job? So there's no way I could persuade you to make a change? OK. Sorry to have taken your time. Thanks anyway. Goodbye."

The young man then hung up and exited the booth. But the man who'd been waiting to use the phone couldn't help expressing his admiration at the younger man's initiative. He also expressed his sympathy that the young man had failed to get the job.

"Better luck next time," he said.

The younger man said, "Thanks, but it's OK. Everything's fine. Actually, that was my own boss I was talking to. I was just checking up on myself to see how I'm doing."

Life will subject each of us to some rigorous tests. Those who are best prepared are those who've already tested themselves.

But who can detect his own failings?
Wash away my hidden faults.
And from pride preserve your servant,
never let it be my master.

PSALM 19:12-13, NJB

One Life

> There's no such thing as a person alone.
> There are only people bound to each other
> to the limits of humanity and time.
>
> MICHEL QUOIST

*C*hicken Soup for the Soul recounts the classic story about a boy picking up a starfish stranded on the beach and tossing it back into the ocean. A man walks by and tells the boy there are so many thousands of starfish that saving just one really doesn't matter. To which the boy replies, "Sir, it matters to this one."

I thought of that familiar story when the Air Force went to such extraordinary lengths to transport urgently needed medical supplies to one woman member of an isolated polar expedition. At the South Pole, it was the dead of winter—impossible for anything to land in the screaming, icy winds, with sixty-seven-degrees-below-zero temperatures and twenty-four-hour darkness.

Yet with night goggles, oxygen masks, and a huge supply of courage, an Air Force crew made a dramatic and successful drop of supplies. They risked their own lives to save just one person. Daily, someplace in the world, people are taking incredible risks to save some individual. An infant stuck in a well; an elderly person trapped in a fire; a pilot downed at sea; a skier marooned on a snowy mountain.

Humans do this because somehow we instinctively understand that every life has intrinsic value and that to save a single life is to save the world. Like the boy saving the starfish, what we do may not seem to matter much. Yet there will be one to whom it matters a great deal.

What is the value of a single life? Is the life of a stranger worth less than your own? Or worth less than the life of someone you love?

O Lord, you have searched me and you know me.
You know when I sit and when I rise;
*   you perceive my thoughts from afar.*
You discern my going out and my lying down;
*   you are familiar with all my ways.*
Before a word is on my tongue
*   you know it completely, O Lord.*

PSALM 139:1-4, NIV

Loving Touch

*T*he woman had decided to end her skin care, makeup, home party business, but her sample cases were not returnable. The products were perfectly good, so she wondered how she should use them.

Why not go to a local retirement home and give a free demonstration? She had done it so many times. Only this time there would be no sales pitch at the end.

She went with a friend, and as they unpacked their supplies, carefully spreading them out on a wooden table in the recreation room, aides went to bring in the residents. One by one the women arrived, most in their eighties and one lady, ninety-one years old. Three were in wheelchairs. Two others used walkers. They seemed very old, but appreciative.

With heads bowed and hands folded, they thanked the women for coming and for giving them something to do. Both women wondered if they had done the right thing. But as they handed out samples of cleansing creams, warm washcloths, and moisturizers, the ladies brightened. How pleasant the creams felt on their faces! And as they chatted, it became clear these ladies weren't as old on the inside as they looked on the outside.

For more than two hours, the makeup women applied sexy eye shadow, dabbed on face powder, lined their dainty, shrunken lips with red lipstick. The activities director oohed and ahhed and told them how sultry, how sexy they looked. Those who could still see, strained to look at themselves in mirrors. And they smiled the most wonderful smiles.

There are few nicer gifts we can give an older person than the gift of feeling young again—if only for a little while.

You were called to be free; do not use your freedom as an open-ing for self-indulgence, but be servants to one another in love, since the whole of the Law is summarized in the one com-mandment: You must love your neighbor as yourself.

GALATIANS 5:13-14, NJB

Good News for a Change

> *If you keep saying things are going to be bad, you have a good chance of being a prophet.*
>
> Isaac Bashevis Singer

With all due respect to some very real problems, the news isn't all gloom and doom. So that our emotions don't get ahead of the facts, let's look at what's real.

The number of students expelled for bringing guns and explosives into schools actually dropped last year dramatically, according to the Education Department. Despite media hysteria, the number of such expulsions was down 31 percent from the previous year. Some states did even better. Ohio, for instance, reported an 87 percent decline.

While news reports may make it feel like everyone either is dying from cancer—or will—the facts tell a different story. Today nearly eight and a half million people have survived cancer and are alive more than five years after diagnosis. That's a 60 percent survival rate, compared to only 51 percent in the early 1980s.

Poverty is at the lowest rate in twenty years. Last year alone more than a million people got off the poverty rolls, even as our population was growing.

Acknowledging progress is important, because unless we recognize that improvement is possible, why would we bother to try?

Despite the often mind-numbing headlines, our world is not spinning crazily out of control. In small, quiet, but important ways, some things are actually getting better.

Bless the Lord, O my soul,
*   and do not forget all his benefits—*
who forgives all your iniquity,
*   who heals all your diseases,*
who redeems your life from the Pit,
*   who crowns you with steadfast love and mercy,*
who satisfies you with good as long as you live
*   so that your youth is renewed like the eagle's.*

PSALM 103:2-5, NRSV

Hero to the Homeless

> *Compassion is the basis of all morality.*
> ARTHUR SCHOPENHAUER

*D*id you know there are well-educated, well-groomed, mentally healthy, middle-class women who are homeless? Who spend their nights on the street, sleeping in parked cars? Who while away their days in libraries or malls, who do their makeup at department store cosmetic counters, and who wash and blow-dry their hair in hotel and restaurant washrooms?

Marjorie Bard knows these women exist, because she used to be one. She escaped from an abusive marriage, but had no place to go. Because she knows about that life so well, she's founded Women Organized Against Homelessness, an organization designed to help such women develop strategies for both survival and eventual return to the mainstream.

Marjorie, who has a Ph.D., spent two years living out of her own car while trying to keep up middle-class appearances. Now she's become an expert in helping other women discover the assistance that's available to them. She shows them the eligibilities and entitlements they usually don't know about.

Marjorie Bard lives with her ailing mother and receives no

money for her work on behalf of the homeless. Yet the satisfaction she receives by helping other women find work, homes, and hope, she says, is compensation enough.

Heroes, like the homeless, wear many faces, not all of them recognizable. Marjorie Bard is such a hero, one of countless Americans who go quietly about the daily business of doing good.

This is how we know what love is: Jesus Christ laid down his life for us. And we ought to lay down our lives for our brothers.
1 JOHN 3:16, NIV

Field of Dreams

> Reach high, for stars lie hidden in your soul. Dream deep, for every dream precedes the goal.
>
> PAMELA VAULL STARR

Dick Davis had farmed all his life. Yet he'd always harbored a secret dream, and so, at age sixty-four, he did something his children considered bizarre. Dick bought a used road grader for $200, drove it onto one of his pastures, and cut two long swaths forming a huge X on the field.

"I'm making an airport," Dick informed his startled sons. "I'm through with farming. I always wanted to fly and I'm turning this land into an airport."

Dick then sold the rest of the farm and got his pilot's license. Eventually, other pilots flying over Dick's little country airport began landing. He would pull out an old stepladder, personally fuel their planes, and clean their windshields.

Dick and his wife served coffee to the pilots. Word of their hospitality spread. After a while, Dick was able to pave the runways. Today, his field of dreams has become one of central Wisconsin's best and busiest.

It was over twenty years ago that Dick Davis cut that X in the pasture. Just *this* year Dick finally retired from flying at the age of eighty-five.

A dream deferred is not necessarily a dream denied. Our dreams die only when we stop feeding them.

Since, then, you have been raised with Christ, set your hearts on things above, where Christ is seated at the right hand of God.

COLOSSIANS 3:1, NIV

Accidental Negatives

> *There ain't but one thing wrong with every one of us, and that's selfishness.*
>
> WILL ROGERS

*I*t was almost picture-perfect. There in the stack of vacation photographs was one of us together. Amazingly, we both liked it. Our eyes were open. We both were smiling. We looked natural. Even thinner. This definitely was a framer. One for the wall. But then we noticed the people in the background.

Call it a negative impression, but they ruined the picture. One was shoveling a forkful of food into what looked like an already full mouth. Another had a contorted look on his face as though he'd been frozen in mid-sneeze. The images were less than flattering. We tossed the photo back into the pile. So much for framing.

Yet the experience did give me second thoughts about the countless impressions we all leave in the background of our lives when we aren't center stage and when, perhaps, we think it doesn't really matter.

Failing to thank the waitress who brings coffee.

Failing to return the receptionist's smile as we wait for an appointment.

Cutting off another motorist in traffic or getting all steamed because someone cut us off. Sometimes you and I can ruin an otherwise perfectly good picture.

You never know what kind of background you're providing. And, even worse, you never know who's got it on film.

Be kind to one another.

EPHESIANS 4:32, NRSV

Never Too Late

> *Opportunities are often things you haven't noticed the first time around.*
>
> CATHERINE DENEUVE

*H*as anybody ever tabulated just how much time and energy we waste bemoaning all those "if onlys" in life? If only I'd taken that job ten years ago. If only I'd started my own business. Bought that stock. Married that special person. If only I'd finished school.

My father was a college dean, and one day a woman he knew was regretting the fact that she'd never completed college. Dad urged her to go back. After all, there are plenty of adults going back to school, taking night courses, correspondence courses, or courses on the Internet.

Yet she was frustrated by one fact: "Dr. Crim, I'm fifty-five years old. Going to school part time, it would take me five years to earn my degree. Why, in five years I'll be sixty."

Dad thought for a moment, then replied, "Tell me, how old will you be in five years if you don't earn your degree?"

Hockey star Wayne Gretzky once said that we miss 100 percent of the shots we never take. It's never too late to shoot for some new goals.

The best response to a missed opportunity is to catch it on its way around the next time.

Moses was eighty years old and Aaron eighty-three when they spoke to Pharaoh.

EXODUS 7:7, NIV

Best-Case Scenarios

Ain't no use putting up your umbrella till it rains.

ALICE CALDWELL RICE

---

*T*he missing child was only two. So everybody in the small Swiss town swung into action.

Firemen from nearby villages joined the search—ninety-five in all—along with the town's entire seventeen-member police force. They pressed into service three tracking dogs. Medics stood by as searchers checked nearby streams. Radio stations broadcast pleas for help, and before long a hundred volunteers from out of town had joined about twenty searchers from the community. Still not a trace of the child.

Finally, in desperation, the searchers called in a Swiss army bicycle unit. Ultimately, however, that really wasn't necessary. About that time they found the toddler, sound asleep in his pajamas under a blanket at his own house in a room that was rarely used. When the parents first noticed him missing, they immediately had notified authorities. Nobody had bothered to check the house.

How many times have you and I gotten into a panic and conjured up worst-case scenarios in our minds, only to discover

---

there really was no problem? How much more serene our lives would be if first we imagined the best and checked out the most innocent possibilities before surrendering to hysteria.

Worry is like a rocking chair. It gives us something to do but doesn't get us anywhere. What a terrible misuse of the imagination.

If you make the Most High your dwelling—
    even the Lord, who is my refuge—
then no harm will befall you,
    no disaster will come near your tent.
For he will command his angels concerning you
    to guard you in all your ways.

PSALM 91:9-11, NIV

Dream On

> *Nothing great was ever achieved without enthusiasm.*
>
> RALPH WALDO EMERSON

*B*ill Gates was making lots of news as we began the new millennium, but here's a story about Gates you may not have heard. Gates and Paul Allen were students and friends at Harvard when the world's very first personal computer came out. It was called the Altair. However, even though the Altair was a breakthrough in computing, it did not have a programming language of its own.

Gates and Allen had a lot of confidence in their programming skills, so they called the manufacturer and said they'd written a programming language that would run on the Altair. They offered to come to the company's headquarters in Albuquerque during semester break and demonstrate it.

However, only after the commitment was made and the appointment set did Gates and Allen actually begin to write the program that they claimed to have created. Allen, acknowledged to be the better programmer of the two, took their program to Albuquerque. Its very first test would be the big test—the demonstration for the Altair company. The programming passed with flying colors. Both Bill Gates and Paul Allen were off on careers that would change the course of history. And, in the process, make both of them enormously wealthy.

Frequently, success is a matter of how much faith you have in your own abilities, because faith in your abilities determines how much risk you're willing to take to be successful.

> *What are human beings that you spare a thought for*
> *them,...*
> *Yet you have made him little less than a god,*
> *you have crowned him with glory and beauty,*
> *made him lord of the works of your hands,*
> *put all things under his feet.*
>
> PSALM 8:4-6, NJB

Hypocrisy's Cousin

> *Being judgmental and condemning is not one of the gifts of the spirit.*
>
> BILLY GRAHAM

Some of us are old enough to remember 1960 and the huge flap during the Kennedy-Nixon race about whether a Catholic could ever be elected president. That debate ended when Kennedy won.

Religion has long been a point of contention in politics. Years ago in the U.S. Senate, it wasn't a Catholic but a Mormon politician who found himself in the eye of a political hurricane, and this politician already had been elected.

It occurred at a time when the Mormon church still allowed the practice of polygamy. Although newly elected Senator Reed Smoot of Utah had only one wife, some of the Senate's more sanctimonious members said that he shouldn't be seated.

Yet Senator Boise Penrose of Pennsylvania knew that some of his colleagues—even though they had only one wife—were known to womanize. So, taking the podium, he looked directly at some of those senators and he said, "Frankly, as for me, I would prefer to have seated beside me in the Senate a polygamist who doesn't polyg rather than a monogamist who doesn't monog."

That ended the debate. Senator Reed Smoot was promptly given his seat.

Prejudice is a first cousin to hypocrisy. The blanket of bigotry we throw over others may be simply a cover for our own shortcomings.

You, therefore, have no excuse, you who pass judgment on someone else, for at whatever point you judge the other, you are condemning yourself, because you who pass judgment do the same things.

ROMANS 2:1, NIV

Teams Work

*V*ince Lombardi believed in talent, training, and discipline. Yet when asked what he considered the number-one quality for winning, the legendary coach said *teamwork*. For each player to care about the others, he said, was the difference between mediocrity and greatness.

After Sir Edmund Hillary became the first ever to reach the top of Mount Everest, he slipped on his way back down and started to fall. Hillary most certainly would have been killed had his guide not immediately dug in his ice ax and, at great risk to himself, braced the rope linking the two men together. The guide refused the label hero, brushing it off with the comment, "Climbers always help each other."

Have you ever noticed how geese always fly together in a V-formation? Scientists claim that the lift each bird receives in this formation from the other's flapping wings adds at least 71 percent to the range they'd have if each bird flew alone.

Wouldn't you think we humans would have as much sense as a goose?

In sports and in life, it takes more than talent and tenacity to win. It takes teamwork. Those who can't get along rarely move along very far.

For just as the body is one and has many members, and all the members of the body, though many, are one body, so it is with Christ.

1 CORINTHIANS 12:12, NRSV

Unlikely Comeback

> *Hardships, poverty, and want are the best incentives, and the best foundation for a person's success.*
>
> BRADFORD MERRILL

*I*f you want to be inspired, pick up the book *Project Girl* by Janet Macdonald. You'll marvel at the achievements of this impoverished girl born in the Brooklyn housing projects—a girl who graduated from high school at age sixteen but was so naive she didn't know she should already have applied to colleges. Kids *she* knew simply didn't go to college.

Today most all her childhood friends are either on drugs or dead. So what happened to Janet? She managed to get into prestigious Vassar College. Spent her junior year in Paris. Then, law school at Cornell and New York University. Then, a journalism degree from Columbia.

Her book details incredible struggles, setbacks, and challenges during her remarkable journey. And that's the point. With motivation and determination, it is possible to break out of the projects and build a life. Janet is convinced that there are lots of really smart kids out there who simply don't recognize their own abilities. So powerful, so persuasive is Janet's book that it's being considered as required reading in New York City high schools.

For all the changes in her life, the one thing Janet won't change is the tattoo of a raging lion on her shoulder. That, she says, was a part of who she was. And still is.

Failure doesn't have to be final. Janet Macdonald's life is a fresh reminder of how spectacular setbacks can be followed by unlikely comebacks for those determined to succeed.

The Lord is close to the brokenhearted
   and saves those who are crushed in spirit.
A righteous man may have many troubles,
   but the Lord delivers him from them all.

PSALM 34:18-19, NIV

Work Ethic

*D*on't you love the way small children take such intense pride in their accomplishments? Recently, our five-year-old grandson could hardly wait to show us his new backward somersault.

The good feelings we have about our accomplishments have little to do with the accomplishments themselves. They result from our attitude toward what we've achieved, whether it's learning to somersault backward or winning the presidency of the United States.

One of America's most famous political families, the Tafts, once encouraged their youngest child to appreciate each family member's accomplishments. When Martha Taft was in grade school, she was asked to introduce herself.

She said, "My name is Martha Bowers Taft. My great-grandfather was president of the United States. My grandfather was a United States senator. My daddy is ambassador to Ireland. And I am a Brownie."

It isn't only our children who need pride in who they are, in what they do, and in what they've achieved. We all do. We all must remember that there is no unimportant work in the world. It all has to be done. If someone is willing to pay us to do it, then the work, no matter how unglamorous, has value. That value entitles us to feel pride when we do the job, whatever it is, when we do it well.

It isn't our work that produces pride, but rather the way we feel about our work.

I remind you to fan into flame the gift of God, which is in you through the laying on of my hands. For God did not give us a spirit of timidity, but a spirit of power, of love and of self-discipline.

2 TIMOTHY 1:6-7, NIV

To Do or Not to Do

If we really want to live, we'd better start at once to try.

W.H. AUDEN

There are all kinds of ways to avoid respon-sibility. Ultimately, avoidance is never satisfying and often disastrous. One favorite for some college students is to hang around after graduation and keep working toward more advanced degrees. This lets them avoid—or at least postpone—dealing with tougher responsibilities.

A college teacher of theater arts tried to bring the problems of Shakespeare's *Hamlet* into contemporary focus by asking students to consider Hamlet's predicament.

This young Danish prince returned from college abroad to find his father dead under suspicious circumstances, his hated uncle running the family business, his mother married to his uncle, and his girlfriend's father in the pay of his uncle. To complete his misery, his girlfriend told him she was pregnant.

Hoping he'd shown a set of circumstances too much for any young man, the teacher asked, "What would you do if you were in Hamlet's situation?"

One young man in the second row promptly replied, "I'd go back for my master's." Life is like a taxi—the meter just

103

keeps on ticking, whether you're moving or standing still. So you might as well get into gear and get on with it.

Idler, go to the ant;
　ponder her ways and grow wise:
no one gives her orders,
　no overseer, no master,
yet all through the summer she gets her food ready,
　and gathers her supplies at harvest time.
How long do you intend to lie there, idler?
　When are you going to rise from your sleep?

PROVERBS 6:6-9, NJB

Success Stories

> *If at first you don't succeed, you're running about average.*
>
> M.H. ALDERSON

There are exceptions to every rule, and instant success is one of those exceptions. Most success is the result of time and effort. The person who becomes a millionaire by winning the lottery or inheriting a fortune from some long-lost relative clearly is the exception.

Andrew Miller qualifies as an exception. He didn't win a lottery or an inheritance, but what he did is just as extraordinary. Miller won the world's richest prize for a single work of fiction, and he did it with his very first novel, which he titled *Ingenious Pain*.

The great poet e.e. cummings followed a path that was more the rule. When a dozen publishers turned down a collection of his poems, cummings published them himself. His dedication page read "No thanks to...," and then he proceeded to list all twelve publishers who had rejected his book.

Walt Disney's career, too, was the rule and not the exception. When Disney submitted his first drawings for publication, he was told he had no artistic talent.

No, instant success definitely is the exception, not the rule.

That's probably a good thing, because it's been my experience that things produced instantly are never quite as good as those produced patiently, over time—whether it's coffee, photographs, relationships, or success.

Success is measured not by the speed of achievement but by the depth of our commitment and the length of our patience.

By faith, Abraham, even though he was past age—and Sarah herself was barren—was enabled to become a father because he considered him faithful who had made the promise. And so from this one man, and he as good as dead, came descendants as numerous as the stars in the sky and as countless as the sand on the seashore.

HEBREWS 11:11-12, NIV

Self-Love

> *Only the person who has faith in himself is able to be faithful to others.*
>
> ERIC FROMM

*H*ow does a person who feels like a nobody start to feel like a somebody?

A Baptist minister with a doctoral degree in analytical psychology has an answer that makes a lot of sense. Dr. James Anderson says you turn nobodies into somebodies by teaching them to *love* themselves.

Amazing how many of us find it difficult to appreciate and respect ourselves. How many of us feel unworthy of our own love. We focus so much on our negative features that we're blinded to our good points.

We may not like the shape of our bodies. Or the sound of our voices. Perhaps we feel clumsy. Intellectually inferior. Inevitably, a counselor has to wade through a lot of mental and emotional garbage to help a *nobody* discover the real and worthwhile person hidden inside.

Mental health professionals recognize that the inability to care about another almost *always* stems from a poor self-image. And loving ourselves begins like any other kind of love—with acceptance. Accepting what we are. Who we are. How we look. How we sound.

This doesn't mean giving up on improvement. Yet improving ourselves should be a *goal*, not a precondition for loving ourselves.

Mae West once quipped, "I never loved another person the way I love myself." The truth is, we're not *likely* to love another person until we love ourselves. We don't become egotists by thinking *too much* of ourselves, but rather by thinking *too little* of others. And why should we expect others to put a higher value on us than *we* do?

God is love,
and whoever remains in love remains in God
and God in him.

1 JOHN 4:16, NJB

Real Humility

> *Get someone else to blow your horn and the sound will carry twice as far.*
>
> WILL ROGERS

*M*ost of the world's truly great people have a genuine humility about them. Oh, I know, there are plenty of famous people who are pompous, conceited, and self-important. But I'm not talking about fame. I'm talking about greatness.

I have in mind great musicians like the composer and pianist Johannes Brahms. After performing two of his piano concertos in Berlin, he attended a dinner in his honor. The host proposed a toast to "the most famous composer." Before the host could get out any more words, Brahms hastily hoisted his glass and shouted, "Quite right. Here's to Mozart!"

On another occasion, Brahms visited a great wine connoisseur. In honor of his distinguished guest, the man had brought out several of his best wines. "This is the Brahms of my cellar," he announced as he poured one particularly choice wine into the great composer's glass.

Brahms went through the tasting ritual, looked closely at the wine, inhaled its bouquet. Then, after sipping it, he placed his glass on the table, turned to his host, and said, "Better bring out your Beethoven."

Every one who exalts himself will be humbled, and he who humbles himself will be exalted.

LUKE 14:11, RSV

Making Opportunities

> *A wise man will make more opportunities than he finds.*
>
> FRANCIS BACON

*T*he young woman had finished college but there were no jobs available in her field. So, she improvised. It occurred to her that while her specialty was oversupplied, there weren't enough good, professional housekeepers to satisfy the market. So, she passed out flyers in a nearby affluent neighborhood and soon had her own business under way. It's not what she plans to do permanently, but she says it beats welfare or unemployment checks. And she feels that she's providing a needed service.

Some aspiring artists in Los Angeles took a similar tack when they were unable to get their paintings shown in the established galleries. Pooling their money, they rented a motel room for sixty-one dollars a night and began showing their works under the heading "One-Night Stand." The investment paid off. Now potential buyers as well as gallery owners are stopping by, checking out their work.

Innovation sometimes breaks through barriers when nothing else can. When the thing you want to do doesn't seem possible, then do something else. The important thing is to do something.

If opportunity is a door, then ingenuity is the key that unlocks it.

She sets about her work vigorously;
her arms are strong for her tasks.
She sees that her trading is profitable,
and her lamp does not go out at night.

PROVERBS 31:17-18, NIV

Kindness Counts

> We are made kind by being kind.
>
> ERIC HOFFER

For every sensational crime that makes the news, myriad acts of kindness and character go unreported. Except for the alertness of an Air Force information specialist, this might have been one of those unnoticed incidents.

Jason Baxter is a senior airman with the Twenty-Fifth Intelligence Squadron at Hurburt Field, Florida. He was driving home from a late-night training flight when he spotted what looked like a book lying in the middle of a well-lit street. It was a book, all right. He had found somebody's day planner, but it contained more than telephone numbers and appointments. Tucked inside was nine thousand dollars in cash.

Jason Baxter could have pocketed the money. No one had seen him pick up the book. Yet Jason says, as a Christian, there was no way he could keep it. Besides, integrity, he says, is one of the Air Force's core values. So, he went to the police and they found the owner—Karrie Jo Blakston.

The nineteen-year-old and her boyfriend had earlier that day withdrawn the cash for their wedding. She'd left it on top of her car and driven away.

The measure of people's integrity is what they do when they think they can get away with it.

The righteous walk in integrity—happy are the children who follow them!

PROVERBS 20:7, NRSV

Choose Happiness

> *Most folks are about as happy as they make up their minds to be.*
>
> ABRAHAM LINCOLN

By any objective standard, life is no more dangerous now than it's ever been. Sure, we have muggings, car wrecks, plane crashes, blizzards, hurricanes, tornadoes, diseases. But, hey, life's always been hazardous to our health. The truth is, our life *expectancy* is way up from what it was at the turn of the century—almost double. Some diseases that terrified and killed our grandparents are practically unheard of today. Certainly our standard of living is higher.

So, if we aren't happier, why aren't we? It's pretty obvious: Happiness isn't produced by circumstances.

It's not what's in our environment, but rather what's in our head. It's the attitude inside, not the atmosphere outside, that determines happiness. I have never met a truly happy person whose happiness was contingent upon what he or she had. Instead, it always had a lot to do with how the person thought, how he or she approached life, and what he or she considered important. It always had a lot to do with how that person balanced expectations and achievement. And whether that person set his or her own standards instead of chasing those of other people.

When it comes to curing dissatisfaction, we have to be our own physicians. Only *we* are qualified to write the prescription that will bring us happiness and contentment.

Set your hearts on his kingdom first, and on God's saving justice, and all these other things will be given you as well.

MATTHEW 6:33, NJB

Along the Way

> *Journeying is more*
> *Than reaching destination.*
> *Journeying is more.*
>
> JEAN FOX HOLLAND

I'm big on goal setting and realizing dreams. So what I'm about to say may sound like a contradiction, but it's not. It's about priorities. *Reaching* goals is important, but it's not the most important thing. *Striving* to reach goals is most important. Sometimes it's process, not result, that counts most.

Two small boys were digging a deep hole behind their house. A couple of older boys stopped to watch. Finally they asked the younger ones what they were doing.

"We're going to dig a hole through the earth," one of them said. "We plan to go all the way to China."

The older boys started laughing. "You guys can't dig through the earth. That's impossible."

After a long silence, one of the smaller lads picked up a jar full of spiders, worms, and an assortment of insects. He removed the lid, showed these wonderful creatures to the scoffing visitors, and said, confidently, "Well, even if we don't dig all the way through the earth, look at the great stuff we found along the way."

It's in the journey, not the destination, that life is lived. When we focus too much on the goal, we miss a lot of interesting stuff along the way.

"Come, follow me," Jesus said.

MATTHEW 4:19, NIV

Moments to Remember

> *A thankful heart is not only the greatest virtue, but the parent of all other virtues.*
>
> CICERO

*O*nce I received a birthday card that contained this line: "We do not remember days, we remember moments."

Think about it. Can we really remember a day? Even yesterday? Our memories are a collage of individual moments: that instant when our exuberant toddler picked up a shell on the beach; the moment we received a phone call from the estranged sister we thought might never call; the sunset we shared as we held the hand of someone we loved. That special moment.

Moments, good and bad, happy and disappointing, are woven into memory to make up the fabric of our years. Memories aren't videotapes. They're snapshots. They freeze for us a particular word or mood. They may reinflict the sharp pain of an argument or rekindle the joy of a letter or a kiss.

When that little son or daughter asks us to read or play or take a walk, that child is offering us a rare chance to create moments. Moments that will become memories. Memories that will last long after the child is grown and our busy schedules aren't so busy anymore.

Life is composed of moments. And, like a superbly prepared meal, we enjoy it more if we savor each bite and relish each distinctive flavor.

O Lord, hear my prayer ...
I remember the days of long ago;
I meditate on all your works
and consider what your hands have done.

PSALM 143:1, 5, NIV

Do It Now

> *He who reigns within himself and rules his passions, desires, and fears is more than a king.*
>
> JOHN MILTON

*W*e know there are some unmistakable characteristics that all successful people share. One of them is the ability to make themselves do things they don't want to do. The word is self-discipline. I've never known anyone successful in business or in relationships who hadn't cultivated this important ability.

And not just to do what they disliked, but to do it when it should be done. Britain's famous nineteenth-century biologist and physician, Thomas Huxley, believed that this ability to do what we don't like is the most valuable lesson we can learn in life. These days, time management consultants continually urge us to do first those jobs we like least. Still, most of us procrastinate.

The principle of "do it now" is just as important in relationships. How often do we delay apologizing even when we know we were wrong simply because apologizing isn't fun? Thomas Lynch spent twenty-five years as an undertaker in a small Michigan town where he oversaw some five thousand burials.

What great life lesson has he learned from all this? He says it's made him want to resolve conflicts more quickly because he has seen people go off to work and not come home.

Some of the greatest insights into life come from those who've seen the most of death. One of those insights is this: Don't ever assume you can do tomorrow what ought to be done today. Don't just do it. Do it now!

Live not by your natural inclinations, but by the Spirit, since the Spirit of God has made a home in you.

ROMANS 8:9, NJB

Doctor Mom

> *Great works are performed not by strength,*
> *but by perseverance.*
>
> SAMUEL JOHNSON

*L*ife got off to a rocky start for Shirley. She was expected to be valedictorian at her rural Tennessee high school, but then her parents divorced and Shirley dropped out of school. She waited tables. Worked the desk at a local motel. Sold some insurance. Eventually, Shirley married a man named Clell. After he returned from Vietnam they had two children. Life might have settled into a humdrum routine, but Shirley would have none of it.

She'd never given up her dream of completing school, but not just high school. Now, thirty years later, Shirley has a new title in front of her name: Doctor. How did this high school dropout manage to earn a medical degree? With courage, determination, and wonderful support from her husband.

Clell says that when Shirley made the decision to enter medicine it was like somebody turned on the light. She passed a G.E.D. test, then took two years of community college, four years of pre-med and, finally, medical school—all the while fulfilling her role as both wife and mother. After three years of residency, Dr. Shirley Trentham plans to set up a family practice in her hometown of Pigeon Forge, Tennessee.

Life is what happens while we're making other plans, and the pursuit of a goal rarely follows a straight line. Yet detours often add interest to an otherwise dull and predictable journey.

May the favor of the Lord our God rest upon us;
establish the work of our hands for us—
yes, establish the work of our hands.

PSALM 90:17, NIV

Real Generosity

Goodness is the only investment that never fails.

HENRY DAVID THOREAU

Sometimes the truest judgment of character isn't rendered during a person's lifetime. For example, Charles Spurgeon was a famous preacher, but he and his wife developed a reputation for stinginess. The Spurgeons lived on a farm, and for years they sold all their eggs, milk, and butter. Neighbors wondered why they never gave any away.

The Spurgeons knew that folks criticized them, but they never responded. Only after both were dead did the truth answer for them. During all those years they had used the farm profits to support two elderly widows whose husbands had been Christian ministers.

Yes, some of a person's best character traits may not be recognized until after they're gone. Take, for instance, Randolph Landgraf, who died in Chilton, Wisconsin, at the age of eighty, where he had spent his last couple of years in a nursing home. Folks knew Randy was a good man. Yet none could have guessed that this quiet, unpretentious World War II veteran would leave nearly four hundred thousand dollars to a church where he had never been a member, to a hospital where he had never been a patient, and to the Calumet County Fair. His niece says he never even cared much for fairs. She figures he just wanted to do something good.

Greed and selfishness are usually loud and easy to recognize. Yet true generosity walks softly and wears many disguises.

When you give alms, your left hand must not know what your right is doing; your almsgiving must be secret, and your Father who sees all that is done in secret will reward you.

MATTHEW 6:3-4, NJB

Putting Things in Perspective

> *Sometimes you just have to look reality in the eye and deny it.*
>
> GARRISON KEILLOR

When I was an anchor for a local TV news program, a viewer told me that she and her husband always wondered, *Should we watch Mort at six o'clock and get indigestion or wait 'til eleven and get insomnia?*

Many viewers are alarmed and disgusted by graphic depictions of violence, crime, and ever-present sex scandals. Some have decided to tune out or turn off.

It's not a good idea to deny reality, but it sure would be a lot healthier if we put it into perspective. The bad and the bizarre are real but they're not typical. National surveys continue to show that after terrorism, crime is the number-one concern of Americans, while statistics show that crime rates are coming down.

Crime is of such concern because it dominates the news. Comedian Wally Cox once said that he developed perspective by putting his newspaper in a drawer for two weeks without reading it. Then he'd take it out, read the headline, and say, "Thank God that's not happening now."

If the news has you down, just remember the first law of

today's journalism: There's nothing so small that it can't be blown out of proportion.

Ever were I to walk in a ravine as dark as death
I should fear no danger, for you are at my side.

PSALM 23:4, NJB

Making Time

> *The passing moment is all we can be sure of; it is only common sense to extract its utmost value from it.*
>
> W. SOMERSET MAUGHAM

*I*n Henry David Thoreau's classic, *Walden*, he shared wonderful thoughts about time—that nonrenewable commodity none of us seems to have enough of these days. He once called time "the stream I go a-fishing in."

Why is it that the more devices we come up with to save time, the less of it we seem to have? The answer is that you can't save time. You can only employ it. We can bank money or stack things on shelves. Yet time walks with us, like our shadow. We use it in a moment or lose it.

Another great thinker, India's pacifist revolutionary Mahatma Gandhi, said, "There is more to life than increasing its speed."

Slowing our pace no doubt would help us get more from our minutes and hours. Like Thoreau, we might benefit by spending more time fishing in a stream, walking through the woods, or breaking our routine to watch a sunset. But save time? Forget it. Every new time-saving device invented is just another way to spend time.

We'll never find time for anything. If we want time, we have to make it.

Be careful then how you live, not as unwise people but as wise, making the most of the time, because the days are evil.

EPHESIANS 5:15-16, NRSV

Priceless Friendship

> *Where the love of God is truly perfected ... a tenderness to all creatures made subject to us will be experienced, and a care felt in us that we do not lessen the sweetness of life in the animal creation.*
>
> JOHN WOOLMAN

A dog is supposed to be our best friend, but sometimes we humans have a chance to return the friendship. Gizmo certainly had been a friend to the Walls family. They loved their ten-year-old black Labrador, especially the children.

But did they love him fifteen hundred dollars worth? That's what the vet said it would cost for surgery and chemotherapy after Gizmo was diagnosed with bone cancer. With the treatment, his prognosis would be good. Without it, Gizmo's days were numbered.

Mom and Dad said that as much as they loved Gizmo, they simply couldn't afford that much money to save him. So the kids came up with a way to raise the needed cash: They would sell their toys. They held a yard sale. The money started coming in, dime by dime at first.

However, when word of the children's sacrificial love

spread, donations began pouring in from all over the country. Ten-year-old Kimberly Walls says selling her toys was an easy choice. After she overheard her dad say they'd just have to have Gizmo put to sleep, Kimberly says the decision wasn't hard at all.

How many adults would sell their favorite toys to help a pet? It may be that our noblest deed is the kindness we show to someone who can *never* repay us.

God blessed them and said to them, "Be fruitful and increase in number; fill the earth and subdue it. Rule over the fish of the sea and the birds of the air and over every living creature that moves on the ground."

GENESIS 1:28, NIV

Real Loyalty

Unless you can find ... loyalty, you cannot find unity and peace in your active living.

JOSIAH ROYCE

*R*eporters called James Carville "Captain Cue Ball," and critics considered him a buffoon, blinded by friendship. Yet even his political enemies had to admire his unswerving loyalty to Bill Clinton.

Loyalty is rare these days. The kind of go-through-the-fire loyalty that defies reason or logic. Loyalty that says, "I'll stick with you simply because you're my friend. Because I made a commitment. Because even if I believe you're wrong, I believe loyalty is right."

There are exceptions, even in pro sports. Steve Yzerman, popular captain of Detroit's Red Wings, has spent his entire career with one team rather than selling his services to the highest bidder.

Broadcasting hasn't been immune to the loyalty lag. Traditionally a correspondent with ABC, NBC, or CBS remained with the network for life. Now, like all free agents, journalists move easily from one network to another in search of the best deal.

Yet the best deal never includes loyalty. You can't buy that with money. All you can do with money is pay the salaries of a research team to study the problem. That is, until they quit to take a better offer.

Loyalty that goes to the highest bidder is loyalty that has no real worth.

Faithful Love and Loyalty join together,
Saving Justice and Peace embrace.
Loyalty will spring up from the earth,
and Justice will lean down from heaven.

PSALM 85:10-11, NJB

Touched by TV

Find the good and celebrate it.

BETTY SHABAZZ

*H*ow would you like to have a job that inspired grateful letters like this one from Atlanta:

"I'm a recovering alcoholic with a painful background. I'm now ten years sober and you give me hope. I pray God keeps you going for years."

Or this one from Spokane, Washington: "My mother is an addict of heroin and cocaine. The main reason I'm writing is to thank you for your time and for making a difference."

And several letters saying, "I live for the moment when you say, 'I love you' because it's the only time all week that I hear someone say I'm loved."

Sound like letters to a social worker? A priest, minister, or rabbi? Actually, these are excerpts from hundreds of letters sent weekly to the cast of the television show *Touched by an Angel,* the show experts said couldn't last a season; the show about love and caring and God's intervention. Now many seasons later, it ranks routinely as the second-most watched show on TV. Recently, one episode came in number-one, even beating out *ER.*

In a media landscape dominated by sex, violence, game shows, and mindless talk, perhaps the success of *this* show about significant life-and-death issues is all the proof we need that miracles do happen.

A few committed producers and courageous program executives are showing that you can do good *and* do good business. They're also proving the media's incredible power to inspire when it chooses to focus on the best rather than the worst.

The light of the eyes rejoices the heart,
and good news refreshes the body.
The ear that heeds wholesome admonition
will lodge among the wise.

PROVERBS 15:30-31, NRSV

Plan Ahead

> *When a person does not know what harbor*
> *he is making for, no wind is the right wind.*
>
> LUCIUS SENECA

*I*sn't it pathetic to watch a person or an organization that has no plan? No clue. Aimless. Directionless. Drifting through life without goal or strategy. Such individuals and institutions rarely accomplish much.

Without a plan there's no way to measure progress. Failure can overtake you before you know it. When asked how a project got to be one year late, an IBM engineer replied, "One day at a time."

Sometimes we don't plan because we mistakenly assume the future will be just like the past, so why bother? That's a fatal mistake, because the future inevitably carries surprises:

The printed program for the Army-Navy football game in November 1944 carried a photo of the USS Arizona with this caption: "Despite claims of air enthusiasts, no battleship has yet been sunk by bombs."

Just eight days later, that very ship—the USS Arizona—was at the bottom of Pearl Harbor, sunk by bombs from Japanese planes.

Failure to plan ultimately is a plan for failure. Even a poor plan is better than no plan at all, because with no plan you have nothing with which to work. Yet a poor plan can be modified and maybe even become a good plan.

[Jesus said:] "Suppose one of you wants to build a tower. Will he not first sit down and estimate the cost to see if he has enough money to complete it? For if he lays the foundation and is not able to finish it, everyone who sees it will ridicule him, saying, 'This fellow began to build and was not able to finish.'"

LUKE 14:28-30, NIV

Taming Anger

*B*ook titles have always fascinated me, and this week I came across a real gem. The book was called *How to Pray After You've Kicked the Dog*. It reminded me of a story I once read about Leonardo da Vinci. While da Vinci was working on the face of Jesus in his masterpiece, "The Last Supper," for some reason he lost his temper with a man. The artist cursed and threatened him, and then returned to his canvas.

A funny thing happened, however. Da Vinci couldn't paint anymore. He found himself unable to continue his work until he put down his brushes, found the man, apologized, and asked forgiveness. The man accepted the apology. Da Vinci returned to his studio and completed the painting.

Anger, inappropriate behavior, hurting another person— these can make it difficult for any of us to work or to function efficiently.

Sometimes the biggest barriers to our success aren't those that someone has put out in front of us. They're the barriers we create inside ourselves by bad actions and poor attitudes.

Often the worst things we do to ourselves are those things we've done to other people.

Be angry but do not sin; do not let the sun go down on your anger.

EPHESIANS 4:26, NRSV

Your Personal Best

> *To aim at the best and to remain essentially ourselves is one and the same thing.*
>
> JANET ERSKINE STUART

*I*f there's one thing that'll ruffle a true Scotsman's skirt, it's to discover his kilt is badly or cheaply made. So many kilts are falling apart these days that the industry has formed a watchdog group. So far, seven of Scotland's one hundred kilt makers have joined the Scottish Kilt-Makers Association, entitling them to install special "quality" labels.

Henry Kissinger is of German descent, not Scottish, but he's always been a stickler for quality.

When he was secretary of state, Kissinger once asked an aide to prepare a report. The aide worked around the clock for several days, then nervously handed in the completed account.

Shortly afterward, Kissinger returned it with a note that read simply, "Redo it."

The aide attacked the project with still greater diligence, then handed Kissinger the second version. Again Kissinger tossed it back to him with a note requesting that he do it again. After this happened a third time, the exasperated aide went in to Kissinger and told him, "Look, I've completed this report three times and this is the best job I can do."

To which Kissinger replied, "In that case, I'll read it now."

One of life's greatest satisfactions is knowing we did our best, whether sewing kilts, shaping foreign policy, or baking a cake. The great taste of excellence and quality lingers long after the sweet taste of an easy job or cheap price has turned sour.

Which of you desires life,
*   and covets many days to enjoy good?*
Keep your tongue from evil,
*   and your lips from speaking deceit.*
Depart from evil, and do good;
*   seek peace, and pursue it.*

PSALM 34:12-14, NRSV

The Power of Empathy

> *The secret of success in society is a certain heartiness and sympathy.*
>
> RALPH WALDO EMERSON

The boss was about as pigheaded as they come, and one day he called all his key executives on the carpet. "You people better get on the ball," he fumed. "I'm tired of the bottlenecks around here."

As they left the meeting, one executive whispered to a colleague, "Aren't necks on bottles always at the top?"

John D. Rockefeller was a different kind of boss. When he was running Standard Oil Company, one of his senior executives made a mistake that cost the company more than two million dollars. Everybody figured Rockefeller would come down on the man like a ton of bricks.

Instead, he called the man in, sat down with a notepad, and wrote across the top of it points in favor of the man. He then listed the man's virtues, including how he'd helped the company make the right decision on other occasions.

An executive who witnessed it said later, "Whenever I'm tempted to rip into someone, I force myself first to sit down and list his or her good qualities. By the time I've finished, my anger is under control. I recommend it to anyone who has to deal with people."

Blowing up may make us *feel* better. Yet it won't get others to *do* better. Steam only makes an engine move when it's harnessed. Unless it's controlled and directed, steam is just useless vapor.

We are God's work of art, created in Christ Jesus for the good works which God has already designated to make up our way of life.

EPHESIANS 2:10, NJB

Room Service

> *The service we render others is the rent we*
> *pay for our room on earth.*
>
> WILFRED GRENFELL

We Americans are a generous people, but we often have trouble figuring out how to express our generosity. For instance, we're troubled by the fact that so much good food is thrown away in restaurants, but perplexed as to how that food might be channeled to those who need it.

Naomi Berman-Potash faced a similar moral dilemma. She is the marketing director for a major Houston Hotel. Naomi read an article about a shelter for battered women having to turn away clients for lack of space. Naomi recognized that her hotel often had unbooked rooms, just sitting there empty, doing no one any good. Could they be used?

At first Naomi's manager thought, *no way*. The presence of abused women would offend other guests. Yet Naomi wouldn't give up.

Working on her own time, she developed a program that would allow abused women to check into hotels without being identified as abused. Eventually, Naomi Berman-Potash's idea caught on with her management. Today, the program has been adopted by more than 125 hotels in New York City, Tampa, and West Palm Beach. Naomi Berman-Potash says she won't stop until her project has become truly national.

Compassion is only an empty word until it's expressed in deeds. One of the most difficult yet most important connections we can make is the connection between good intentions and good results.

Pure, unspoilt religion, in the eyes of God our Father, is this: coming to the help of orphans and widows in their hardships, and keeping oneself uncontaminated by the world.

JAMES 1:27, NJB

Remodeled Life

*I*n Detroit during the winter of 1995, Yolanda was in the middle of a divorce and expecting her third child. Both of her parents were dead. She had no money. Life looked bleak.

When the baby arrived he was developmentally disabled. With no husband, no job, and now three children to care for, including one with special needs, Yolanda might have been out of hope—except for two things: determination and her faith in God.

Detroit was offering run-down, tax-delinquent homes for one dollar to anyone who'd fix them up. Yolanda got a friend to baby-sit, and with a thermos of coffee, a blanket, and a book, camped out all night to be at the head of the line.

Her sister, Sherronda, recalls that until that moment, Yolanda had never had a tool in her hand. But she started watching the Home & Garden channel and reading books on home repair. Gradually, she converted that run-down old house into a place of beauty. Friends from church recently put on the finishing touches at a sanding and painting party.

Creating a home for her kids was only the beginning. Yolanda is just as determined to remodel her life and eventually to establish an organization to help other women realize their dreams. She wants to help them realize that it is possible to beat the odds.

In every community across America, countless numbers of single moms are quietly and heroically struggling for their families and for their dreams. We need to recognize them and appreciate them more than we do.

Only faith can guarantee the blessings that we hope for, or prove the existence of realities that are unseen.

HEBREWS 11:1, NJB

Just Do Something

*T*he crucial difference between achievers and nonachievers is not a roll of the dice. Achievers act decisively while others merely talk about it. People who think success is a matter of dumb luck usually are people who've failed.

Successful people know better. They know that action, hard work, and energy—not fate—results in achievement. They don't worry about luck and they don't whine about how fortune has smiled on the other guy.

Someone gave me a timely warning a few years ago and I have it taped near my desk. It says: "Planning to write is not writing. Thinking about writing is not writing. Talking about writing is not writing. Researching to write; outlining to write; none of this is writing. Writing is writing."

That's an important principle that is valid no matter what we do for a living. Doing is doing.

When a famous author was asked if he wrote only when inspired, I heard him say, "You bet I do. And I make sure I'm inspired every morning between eight and eleven."

The best thought-out plan in the world is useless until it's implemented. The difference between achievers and non-achievers is a simple two-letter word: *Do.*

Whatever you do, do it all for the glory of God.
>   1 CORINTHIANS 10:31, NIV

Follow Your Star

> *Nothing splendid has ever been achieved except by those who dared believe that something inside them was superior to circumstances.*
>
> BRUCE BARTON

*I*mitation may be the sincerest form of flattery to the person imitated, but for the one doing the imitating, it's a poor substitute for originality. I heard one of those Elvis impersonators the other day. He had a great voice and lots of talent. I wondered why he hadn't simply tried to develop who he was instead of attempting to be someone else.

The great artist Picasso once recalled how his mother had told him, "Child, if you become a soldier, you'll be a general. If you become a monk, you'll end up as pope." Instead, Picasso says, he became a painter and wound up Picasso.

To follow one's own star requires self-confidence.

A professor stood before his class in organic chemistry and told the twenty seniors: "I know you've all worked hard and many of you will be off to medical school next year. So as not to mess up anybody's grade point average, I'm offering you a deal. Anyone who opts out of today's exam automatically gets a B for the course."

Many students cheered. Most thanked the professor, picked up their books, and walked out. To the few remaining students, the professor said, "I'm so glad to see that you folks believe in yourself. You all have automatic A's."

There is no shortcut to finding ourselves. Each of us has to carve a trail through the wilderness of what others *think* we are to discover what we *really* are.

The lamp of the body is the eye. It follows that if your eye is clear, your whole body will be filled with light.

MATTHEW 6:22, NJB

Second Chances

When he was basketball coach at DePaul University, Ray Meyer delivered the fans winning teams for forty-two consecutive seasons. At one point DePaul had won twenty-nine straight home court games.

Somebody asked Ray how he'd feel if he lost a game after such an impressive streak. He said he'd feel great, because then he could start concentrating on winning instead of on not losing.

There is a difference. Winners aren't people who never lose. They're people who simply get up one more time than they fall down. They play the percentages and manage to rack up a few more victories than defeats.

A woman was incensed to see her name one morning on the obituary page. She stormed into the office of the editor and shouted that this kind of mistake could ruin her career, not to mention the embarrassment it would cause her. The editor tried to apologize, but nothing he could say calmed the irate woman. Finally, he had a suggestion.

"Look, here's what I'll do," he said. "Tomorrow I'll put your name in the birth announcements and that should give you a fresh start."

Well, a fresh start is what all of us need from time to time, because winning streaks never last forever.

Everybody either has messed up or will. Winners are not people who've never stumbled. They're simply people who've refused to stay down.

If we acknowledge our sins,
he is trustworthy and upright,
so that he will forgive our sins
and will cleanse us from all evil.

1 JOHN 1:9, NJB

Conquering Inner Space

> *There must be more to life than having everything.*
>
> MAURICE SENDAK

This is a great time to be alive—more or less. We have so much more of some things and so much less of others.

For instance, does it ever feel like we have more conveniences, but less time? More knowledge, but less judgment? Fancier houses, but weaker families?

Doesn't it sometimes feel like we've added more years to our lives, but not more life to our years? That while we've conquered outer space, we haven't found inner peace?

That we're long on quantity, but short on quality? That we live in a time when the show windows of our existence are full and flashy, but the stockrooms are pitifully empty? Why is it that we seem to have:

More experts, but fewer solutions.

More medicines, but less well-being.

More leisure, but less fun.

More laughter, but less joy.

More academic degrees, but less common sense.

More acquaintances, but fewer friends.

Yes, this is a great time to be alive—more or less—if we can just figure out how to get the more and the less into better balance.

Experience confirms that more is *not* always better. The quality of our lives is determined not by what we have, but by what we appreciate.

Lay up for yourselves treasures in heaven, where neither moth nor rust consumes and where thieves do not break in and steal.

MATTHEW 6:20, RSV

Clear Vision

Adversity causes some men to break, others to break records.

WILLIAM A. WARD

*T*ravis Freeman is a straight-A student at Corbin High in Corbin, Kentucky, a member of the National Honor Society, and a center for the Corbin Redhounds football team. The coach says he's also a major motivator. During a practice sprint recently, Travis ended up pulling another player to the finish, yelling at him, "Pick it up, Ken. Don't give in to it. Pick it up."

Now a high school athlete who's also a good scholar and an outstanding leader might not be that unusual, except for one fact: Travis Freeman is blind. He lost his eyesight at age twelve to bacterial meningitis. He had played football in fifth and sixth grade, however, and wasn't about to let a little thing like blindness stop him.

So there he is, a guy who can't see the goalposts, his teammates, or his opponents, snapping the ball, then blasting ahead, blocking anybody in his way. Teammates occasionally shout directions to Travis, but mostly he plays by instinct. One thing his opponents have learned: Never try a fake on Travis Freeman. It won't work.

The goals we see with our minds often can overcome the obstacles we see with our eyes. The trick is to focus on the goals, not the barriers.

He has sent me to proclaim release to the captives and recovery of sight to the blind.

LUKE 4:18, NRSV

Moving On

Nothing brings home to us the changes in our lives like bringing out old photo albums. Hairstyles, neckties, dresses, even the automobiles. Was life ever really like that? Were we really like that? Yet it isn't only our looks. We change in many ways. Attitudes. Opinions. Knowledge.

Robert Browning was one of the great British poets of the nineteenth century. He was known for the complexity of his themes and his dramatic verse. Browning would meditate ceaselessly on the varieties of human emotions and motivations, so much so that his words could exhaust his readers.

One of his works, "Sordello," was published in 1830. Although the story line is rather simple, Browning's treatment was complicated by his attention to the development of the human soul. Many readers simply couldn't follow it at all.

Finally, the London Poetry Society asked Browning if he would come before them and interpret what he'd written. Browning did. He read a particularly difficult passage aloud. Then he reread it. Then he read it again.

Finally, he offered his explanation. It went like this:

"When I wrote that, God and I knew what it meant. But now, God alone knows."

If only we spent as much time moving on from the past as we spend trying to defend and explain it. We're certainly accountable for past actions, but we don't have to be imprisoned by them. Sometimes we can simply say, "I can't imagine what I was thinking," and then move on.

You were taught to put away your former way of life, your old self, corrupt and deluded by its lusts, and to be renewed in the spirit of your minds, and to clothe yourselves with the new self, created according to the likeness of God in true righteousness and holiness.

EPHESIANS 4:22-24, NRSV

Experience Rules

No amount of reading and intelligent deduction could supplant the direct experience.

JOHN FOWLES

*T*ypically, those with the best education and most training have the best chance of staying employed. Yet college doesn't necessarily assure success.

Walking into a new job with a degree doesn't guarantee that the graduate knows how to do anything. When a recent marketing major showed up for the first day at his new manufacturing position, the boss asked him to sweep the factory floor. The young man protested, "But I'm a college graduate." To this the boss replied, "I forgot. Here, give me the broom and I'll show you how."

Of the wealthiest entrepreneurs in America, more than one in four never got past high school. Fewer than half finished college. They simply have a drive to succeed that overcomes lack of education.

Billionaire Bill Gates is a college dropout. Dave Barry says that while Bill's buddies were frittering away their brainpower studying the French Impressionist Masters, Bill was out making money. Now, Barry says, Bill *hires* French Impressionist masters to paint his garage.

Education may prepare us to make a *life*, but not necessarily to make a *living*. Success in the real world often depends upon skills and qualities you don't always pick up in school.

By wisdom a house is built,
  and through understanding it is established;
through knowledge its rooms are filled
  with rare and beautiful treasures.

PROVERBS 24:3-4, NIV

Diligence Pays

> *They conquer who believe they can.*
>
> JOHN DRYDEN

*T*his story happened many years ago but carries an important message for anyone today worried about a lack of qualifications. It tells about a student seeking a part-time job to help pay his way through Stanford University. At one place where he applied, the manager told him there was only one position available and that was for a typist. The young man said he'd love to take the job, but wouldn't be able to start until the following Wednesday.

The manager agreed and the following Wednesday morning the student arrived, bright and early and ready to work. The manager said, "I like your enthusiasm and your promptness. But I do have one question. Why couldn't you start until today?"

The young man said, "Well, I had to find a typewriter and learn how to use it."

Perhaps it is not surprising that this young man with such self-confidence and determination would later reach the pinnacle of politics. The student's name was Herbert Hoover.

George Bernard Shaw once said that when he was a young man, he noticed that nine out of ten things he did were failures. He didn't want to be a failure. So, he simply did ten times more work.

The sluggard craves and gets nothing,
  but the desires of the diligent are fully satisfied.

PROVERBS 13:4, NIV

Shared Dreams

*I*f you're feeling low-energy today, maybe you have a *dream* deficiency.

In *Chicken Soup for the Soul,* Virginia Satir recounted working with a group of welfare recipients in a poor, southern county. Virginia knew the power of a dream. Yet one woman asked, "What good's a dream when the rats are eating up my kids?"

A man in the group volunteered to repair the woman's screen door so the rats couldn't get in. The woman felt better and the man felt good that he'd helped. Virginia said, "OK, folks, now it's time to dream."

When one woman said her dream was to become a secretary, another offered to keep the woman's six kids a couple of days a week so she could attend community college. Eventually, the woman did become a secretary.

The woman who had cared for the children became a licensed foster care mom. The man who had fixed the screen door became a full-time handyman.

Within twelve weeks, every one of those folks was off welfare, because someone showed them how to tap the incredible power of a dream.

The only thing more powerful than a dream is a dream that's shared.

Be devoted to one another in brotherly love. Honor one another above yourselves.... Share with God's people who are in need. Practice hospitality.

ROMANS 12:10, 13, NIV

Uncommon Sense

A human resources manager once shuffled through some old personnel reports and came across this notation scribbled onto a job application: "He's keenly analytical and his highly developed mentality could best be utilized in research and development. But he lacks common sense."

Computers and calculators, for all the sophisticated work they can perform, simply can't replace old-fashioned common sense. They can't now and never will.

Common sense isn't something we learn in school. That's why some young people seem to be educated beyond their abilities. You don't need an advanced degree to live a happy and successful life. What you need is common sense, the wisdom that has brought meaning throughout the generations to both simple and sophisticated alike. The common sense to live every day to the fullest. To be kind to your neighbor. To be loyal to your family. Generous to others. To be positive and build your life on trust, not fear, anger, or revenge. Work hard. Take care of small things. Nothing complicated, really. Just common sense.

Common sense isn't very common. It's so rare that the person today who shows even the slightest amount of it is often considered wise.

Reverence for the Lord is the foundation of true wisdom.
The rewards of wisdom come to all who obey him.

PSALM 111:10, NLT

Full Cycle

> *What care I though I have not much, I have as much as I desire, if I have as much as I want; I have as much as the most, if I have as much as I desire.*
>
> ARTHUR WARWICK

An American businessman was walking along the dock of a Mexican coastal village when he noticed a fisherman whose boat contained several large-fin tuna. The American complimented him on the quality of his catch, then asked what the man did when he wasn't fishing.

"Oh," he said, "I sleep late, fish a little, play with my children, take siesta with my wife, Maria. Then each evening we stroll into the village where I play guitar with my amigos. I have a full, busy life, senor."

The American scoffed, "Look, I'm a Harvard MBA. I could help you build a fishing business. If you were willing to work harder and fish longer, in about twenty years you could have an entire fleet of boats. You could open your own processing plant and cannery. Then you could leave this village, move to Mexico City, and run your empire."

The fisherman asked, "Then what?"

"Why then," the American said, "you could announce an IPO, sell your company, and make millions."

"Then what?" the fisherman wanted to know.

"Why, then, you could retire, move to a small coastal village, sleep late, fish a little, take siesta with your wife, stroll to the village in the evenings and play guitar with your amigos."

Having a full schedule doesn't guarantee a full life. Making good time is less important than making our time good.

Can all your worries add a single moment to your life? Of course not.

MATTHEW 6:27, NLT

Top Ten Sayings

> *Common sense, in an uncommon degree, is what the world calls wisdom.*
>
> SAMUEL TAYLOR COLERIDGE

*D*aniel Starch, a business research consultant, has come up with a list of America's favorite sayings. You could call it our top ten principles for living:

10. An ounce of prevention is worth a pound of cure.
9. Actions speak louder than words.
8. Knowledge is power.
7. As a man thinks in his heart, so is he.
6. The only way to have a friend is to be one.
5. The great essentials of happiness are something to do, something to love, and something to hope for.
4. If at first you don't succeed, try, try again.
3. Anything that's worth doing at all is worth doing well.
2. Know yourself.

And the number-one favorite saying of Americans is the Golden Rule: Do unto others as you would have others do unto you.

The principles for successful living are like the physical laws governing nature—they never change. The only thing that changes is our understanding of them.

> *And now, O Israel, what does the Lord your God ask of you but to fear the Lord your God, to walk in all his ways, to love him, to serve the Lord your God with all your heart and with all your soul, and to observe the Lord's commands and decrees that I am giving you today for your own good?*
>
> DEUTERONOMY 10:12-13, NIV

Letting Go

> *Life is 10 percent what you make it and 90 percent how you take it.*
>
> IRVING BERLIN

*L*etting go is one of life's toughest challenges. Letting go of the child, struggling its way into adulthood. Letting go of a loved one, being snatched from us by divorce or death.

Letting go is a hard but necessary part of life. It doesn't mean cutting ourselves off. It does mean realizing that we can't control other people and that we can't always control life.

To let go is to admit powerlessness, which means the outcome isn't always in our hands.

To let go is not to blame or try to change another. We can only change ourselves.

To let go is not to judge, but to allow another to be a human being.

To let go is not to be protective, but to permit another to face reality.

To let go is not to deny, but to accept.

To let go is not to nag, scold, or argue, but to search out our own shortcomings and correct them.

To let go is not to adjust everything to our desires, but to take each day as it comes and to cherish the moment.

To let go is to fear less and to love more.

To let go is to stop regretting the past and start growing and living for the future.

Trust in the Lord, and do good;
   so you will live in the land, and enjoy security.
Take delight in the Lord,
   and he will give you the desires of your heart.

PSALM 37:3-4, NRSV

How to Change the World

> *To live is to change, and to be perfect is to change often.*
>
> JOHN HENRY NEWMAN

*R*emember the song, "If I Ruled the World?" The writer figured things would go a lot better if he were in charge. Yet fantasizing about what we *would* do if we had unlimited power is a cop-out. What about the power we have?

Consider these words on the tomb of an Anglican bishop in the crypts of Westminster Abbey.

When I was young and my imagination had no limits, I dreamed of changing the world.

As I grew older and wiser, I discovered the world would not change. So I shortened my sights and decided to change only my country.

But it, too, seemed immovable.

As I grew into my twilight years, in one last desperate attempt, I settled for changing only my family, but alas, they would have none of it.

And now as I lie on my deathbed, I suddenly realize: If I had only changed myself, first, then by example I would have changed my family.

From their inspiration and encouragement, I would have been able to better my country and—who knows—I may even have changed the world.

Never underestimate the power of a single act. Even the smallest change can have effects more far-reaching than we ever dreamed. The most effective change begins within.

You have stripped off the old self with its practices and have clothed yourselves with the new self, which is being renewed in knowledge according to the image of its creator.

COLOSSIANS 3:9-10, NRSV

Other books in the Good News series

by Mort Crim

Good News for a Change

The Joy of Good News

AVAILABLE AT YOUR LOCAL BOOKSTORE

SERVANT PUBLICATIONS